PENGUIN  CLASSICS

THE BERNARD SHAW LIBRARY

SAINT JOAN

'He did his best in redressing the fateful unbalance between truth and reality, in lifting mankind to a higher rung of social maturity. He often pointed a scornful finger at human frailty, but his jests were never at the expense of humanity' Thomas Mann

'Shaw will not allow complacency; he hates second-hand opinions; he attacks fashion; he continually challenges and unsettles, questioning and provoking us even when he is making us laugh. And he is still at it. No cliché or truism of contemporary life is safe from him' Michael Holroyd

'In his works Shaw left us his mind . . . Today we have no Shavian wizard to awaken us with clarity and paradox, and the loss to our national intelligence is immense' John Carey, *Sunday Times*

'An important writer and an interesting socialist and critic . . . Thank God he lived' Peter Levi, *Independent*

'He was a Tolstoy with jokes, a modern Dr Johnson, a universal genius who on his own modest reckoning put even Shakespeare in the shade' John Campbell, *Independent*

'His plays were superb exercises in high-level argument on every issue under the sun, from feminism and God, to war and eternity, but they were also hits – and still are' Paul Johnson, *Daily Mail*

BERNARD SHAW was born in Dublin in 1856. Although essentially shy, he created the persona of G.B.S., the showman, satirist, controversialist, critic, pundit, wit, intellectual buffoon and dramatist. Commentators brought a new adjective into English: Shavian, a term used to embody all his brilliant qualities.

After his arrival in London in 1876 he became an active Socialist and a brilliant platform speaker. He wrote on many social aspects of the day: on *Common Sense about the War* (1914), *How to Settle the Irish Question* (1917) and *The Intelligent Woman's Guide to Socialism and Capitalism* (1928) published by Penguin. He undertook his own education at the British Museum and consequently became keenly interested in cultural subjects. Thus his prolific output included music, art and theatre reviews, which were collected into several volumes, such as *Music In London 1890–1894* (3 vols., 1931); *Pen Portraits and Reviews* (1931); and *Our Theatres in the Nineties* (3 vols., 1931). He also wrote five novels, including *Cashel Byron's Profession*, and a collection of shorter works issued as *The Black Girl in Search of God and Some Lesser Tales* (also in Penguin).

Shaw conducted a strong attack on the London Theatre and was closely associated with the intellectual revival of British Theatre. His many plays (the full canon runs to 52) fall into several categories: 'Plays Pleasant'; 'Plays Unpleasant'; 'Plays for Puritans'; political plays; chronicle plays; 'metabiological Pentateuch' (*Back to Methuselah*) in five plays; extravaganzas; romances; and fables. He died in 1950.

IMOGEN STUBBS was educated at Oxford and RADA among other places. She has contributed numerous articles to many newspapers and magazines – often in the form of book reviews for *The Times* and travel articles for *Harpers and Queen* and *Conde Naste Traveller*. Her story 'The Undiscovered Road' was recently published in *Amazonians: The Penguin Book of New Women's Travel Writing*. She also acts, swing dances, has a family and is learning the saxophone.

JOLEY WOOD was educated at the University of Wisconsin and received his M.Phil. in Anglo-Irish Literature from Trinity College, Dublin. He now works as a teacher, and freelance writer and editor. He has written on many twentieth-century Irish writers, particularly James Joyce and *Ulysses*, and has edited a number of other works. He is currently writing entries on Irish literature for the *Encyclopaedia of Ireland* (Gill and Macmillan Press).

DAN H. LAURENCE, editor of Shaw's *Collected Letters*, his *Collected Plays with their Prefaces*, *Shaw's Music* and (with Daniel Leary) *The Complete Prefaces*, was Literary Adviser to the Shaw Estate until his retirement in 1990. He is Series Editor for the works of Shaw in Penguin.

BERNARD SHAW

Saint Joan

A Chronicle Play in Six Scenes and an Epilogue

Definitive text under the editorial supervision of
DAN H. LAURENCE
with 'On Playing Joan' by IMOGEN STUBBS
and an Introduction by JOLEY WOOD

PENGUIN BOOKS

PENGUIN BOOKS

Published by the Penguin Group
Penguin Books Ltd, 80 Strand, London WC2R ORL, England
Penguin Putnam Inc., 375 Hudson Street, New York, New York 10014, USA
Penguin Books Australia Ltd, 250 Camberwell Road, Camberwell, Victoria 3124, Australia
Penguin Books Canada Ltd, 10 Alcorn Avenue, Toronto, Ontario, Canada M4V 3B2
Penguin Books India (P) Ltd, 11 Community Centre, Panchsheel Park, New Delhi – 110 017, India
Penguin Books (NZ) Ltd, Cnr Rosedale and Airborne Roads, Albany, Auckland, New Zealand
Penguin Books (South Africa) (Pty) Ltd, 24 Sturdee Avenue, Rosebank 2196, South Africa

Penguin Books Ltd, Registered Offices: 80 Strand, London WC2R ORL, England

www.penguin.com

The play first produced in New York 1923; in London 1924
First published 1924
First published in Penguin Books 1946
Reprinted with 'On Playing Joan' and a new Introduction in Penguin Classics 2001
Reissued with a new Chronology 2003
10

Set in 10.25/12.25 pt PostScript Adobe Sabon
Typeset by Rowland Phototypesetting Ltd, Bury St Edmunds, Suffolk
Printed in England by Clays Ltd, St Ives plc

Contents

Chronology of the Life and Times of Bernard Shaw

LIFE

1856 Born in Dublin on 26 July

1871 After only short periods of schooling, started work as an office boy in a Dublin firm of land agents

1873 Mother and sisters moved to London

1876 Joined mother in London; she taught singing and his sister Lucy sang professionally in musical plays

1879 While working for the Edison Telephone Company, began to meet the earliest British socialists, including, in 1880, Sidney Webb and Beatrice Potter (later Mrs Webb) who became lifelong friends

1879–81 Wrote five novels, four published serially in magazines

1884 Joined the Fabian Society, which advocated gradual progress towards socialism, and began giving lectures both to the Fabians and on their behalf. At about the same time, met the hugely influential theatre critic William Archer, who helped Shaw to find work as a critic. First meeting with William Morris whose disciple he became

1885 Appointed as a book reviewer for the *Pall Mall Gazette* and music critic for the new *Dramatic Review*

1886–9 Art critic for *The World*

1888–90 Music critic for *The Star* (under the pseudonym 'Corno di Bassetto')

1889 Attended English première of Henrik Ibsen's *A Doll's House*

1890–4 Music critic for *The World* (writing as GBS)

1891 Published *The Quintessence of Ibsenism*

1892 *Widowers' Houses* (his first published play) given a private performance by the Independent Theatre in London

1894 *Arms and the Man* produced at the Avenue Theatre in London; then by actor-manager Richard Mansfield in New York

1895–8 Drama critic for *The Saturday Review*

1897 Encouraged by the success of *The Devil's Disciple* in New York, gave up most of his work as a critic

1897–1903 Elected borough councillor for the London borough of St Pancras

1898 *Plays Pleasant and Unpleasant* published. Married Charlotte Payne-Townshend. Began concentrating on his writing as playwright and essayist

1899 The newly founded Stage Society produced *You Never Can Tell*, followed by *Candida* and *Captain Brassbound's Conversion* in 1900

1904–7 Granville Barker and Vedrenne take over the (Royal) Court Theatre in a challenge to the commercial West End theatre system. Eleven Shaw plays produced at the Court including the newly written *Man and Superman, John Bull's Other Island, Major Barbara* and *The Doctor's Dilemma*

1905 Bought a country home at Ayot St Lawrence, approximately 25 miles north of London (retaining an apartment in Adelphi Terrace, off the Strand)

1910 *Misalliance* produced at the Duke of York's Theatre

1913 *Androcles and the Lion* at St James's Theatre. World première of *Pygmalion* in Vienna (in German), followed by a production in Berlin

1914 *Pygmalion* produced by Herbert Beerbohm Tree, at His Majesty's Theatre. *Common Sense about the War* published

1920 *Heartbreak House* produced at the Royal Court. Completed *Back to Methuselah*, a five-part cycle of plays, transforming the biblical version of creation and human destiny into post-Darwinian science fiction

1924 *Saint Joan* produced at the New Theatre

1925 Awarded the Nobel Prize for Literature. First English public performance of *Mrs Warren's Profession* (banned by the censor since 1898)

1928 Published *The Intelligent Woman's Guide to Socialism and Capitalism*

1929 *The Apple Cart*, produced at the first Malvern Festival, organized by Barry Jackson's Birmingham Repertory Theatre with Shaw as its figurehead

1931 Visited Moscow, and met Stanislavski, Gorki and Stalin

1932 *Too True to be Good* produced at Malvern. Published fable of *The Adventures of the Black Girl in Her Search for God* following a visit to South Africa

1933 Travelled to India, Hong Kong, China, Japan and the USA

1936 Celebrated 80th birthday. Gave up driving

1938 Awarded Oscar for the best screenplay for Gabriel Pascal's film of *Pygmalion*. *Geneva* (featuring caricatures of Hitler and Mussolini called before the International Court of Justice at the Hague) transferred from Malvern to Saville Theatre, and then to St James's Theatre

1939 Ceremonially presented with the deeds of a site (in South Kensington) for the National Theatre of Great Britain

1943 Death of Charlotte Shaw

1944 Published *Everybody's Political What's What?*, an instant best-seller

1946 On his 90th birthday, honoured with the freedom of both Dublin and the borough of St Pancras

1950 Died on 2 November

1955 Alan J. Lerner based the book and lyrics of the musical *My Fair Lady* closely on *Pygmalion*

TIMES

1856 End of the Crimean War. Sigmund Freud born

1859 Charles Darwin's *On the Origin of Species* published. Construction of the Suez Canal started

1861–5 American Civil War

1866 The Fenians, Irish Republicans, opposed the English occupation of Ireland

1867 Karl Marx's *Das Kapital* and Matthew Arnold's 'Dover Beach' published

1870 Education Act made primary schooling compulsory in England and Wales

1871 Year of political change in Europe: Italy and Germany both unified

1883 Death of Marx. The left-wing Fabian Society founded

1886 Home Rule for Ireland first proposed by Gladstone's Liberal government; the Conservative Lord Salisbury became Prime Minister

1887 Queen Victoria celebrated her Golden Jubilee

1892 Keir Hardie elected as first Independent Socialist Member of Parliament

1895 Oscar Wilde imprisoned for homosexual offences. Lumière brothers patented cinematograph

1897 Irish Literary Theatre founded by W. B. Yeats, Lady Gregory and Edward Martyn

1899–1902 Anglo-Boer War in South Africa

1901 Death of Queen Victoria, accession of Edward VII

1907 Rudyard Kipling the first British winner of the Nobel Prize for Literature

1911 Members of Parliament paid a salary for the first time. Women's Freedom League founded

1914–18 First World War

1916 Easter Rising by Irish Nationalists in Dublin

1920 League of Nations created. Government of Ireland Act, partitioning Ireland

1922 Continuing civil war in Ireland

1924 First Labour government in Britain, under Ramsay Macdonald; replaced by the Conservative Unionists, under Stanley Baldwin. Death of Lenin

1928 Women over twenty-one in the United Kingdom given the vote

1929 New York Stock Exchange crash led to world economic depression. Election of second Labour minority government in Britain (which became a multi-party National government in 1931)

1933 Adolf Hitler became Chancellor of Germany

1939–45 Second World War

1945 Labour Party, under Clement Attlee, won the election, replacing the wartime leader Winston Churchill.

1946 First meeting of the General Assembly of the United Nations

1948 British National Health Service founded

'On Playing Joan'

by Imogen Stubbs

A leading actress shares her personal memories of the challenges to be found in playing Joan, mirroring the sense of fun in Joan herself and in much of Shaw's play.

When the part of Shaw's Joan was first proposed to me, it set me thinking about the audience expectations of a play called *Saint Joan*, written by an Anglo-Irishman in the 1920s about a dead French girl who had just been canonized for her efforts to get the English out of France several hundred years previously.

It sounded like a dead tree on a lonely road. I'd 'done' *Saint Joan* at school – I'd seen the statue, so to speak. The words 'not relevant' kept singing in my head (along with 'Didn't the 47-year-old Sybil Thorndike, to whom I bear no resemblance, play her "definitively?"'). Having toured the play around Britain and into the West End, I think – I hope – I was quite wrong about the relevance of the play (though probably not about Sybil Thorndike).

One is wary of being an apologist for Shaw when he is such a great apologist for himself, but by placing himself as an amused observer of human endeavour, his arguments are as provocative now – in a society which, for instance, still struggles with the notion of the ordination of women priests – as they were when he wrote the play.

But (rather obviously) what greatly fascinates me is the story of Joan – the Cinderella with a 'Ready-Brek' glow, yes, but also the intractable teenager with the intolerance of youth and the naiveté and dogged determination of a child; a woman who was burned to death at an age when most people's lives have hardly begun.

Shaw presents a girl who has an anarchic sense of humour, who is sometimes hard, violent, hysterical, proud, serene, vulnerable, always courageous. He is accountable to her, and he requires the same loyalty from the actress who plays Joan, to whom he also entrusts the difficult task of playing 'Faith' as a quality of life.

The play presents two other practical challenges to an actress. One is coping with the fact that your fellow actors cannot resist hiding speakers on stage, so in the middle of a big speech you might suddenly hear a muddled: 'Hey, Joanie – it's me Saint Catherine. Can you hear me?' The other is, miracle of miracles, the wind changing. This requires a banner, a wind machine, and a sense of humour. We had nightmares with that moment. The poor boy whose only line was to leap up and down and shout 'The wind! The wind! – It's CHANGED!' would either have to scream above the sound of a Boeing 707 taking off, or stare at the limp banner and say 'The wind! The wind! I'm sure it's about to change', rush into the wings screaming 'Point the machine higher you idiots' and then rush back on stage and say 'God has spoken'.

I once played a character called Anna Lee in a television series which attracted a certain following of young teenage girls who, in their much-appreciated devotion, came to see *Saint Joan* with no prior knowledge of the play and much trepidation that their hard-saved pennies were about to be squandered.

What I found so rewarding (and a relief) was that these girls generally seemed to respond to the character of Joan. Variously – and rather surprisingly – they said that they saw something in Joan of Anne Frank, of the boy in *ET*, of Kenneth Branagh's Henry V. But, overwhelmingly, they saw a heroine who was killed for many of the choices that they took for granted.

They saw a teenager whose combustible combination of naïvety and raw presumption led her to fight passive acceptance of chauvinism and the status quo; someone who believed in spiritual forces greater than the self-appointed ones on earth; a loner, whose journey seems to be one suffered by many teenage icons – defiant, proud, alone, sad, disillusioned, dead and then celebrated. They saw someone who saved her country, only to be burned at the stake because any girl with cropped short hair wearing trousers and clompy boots, any girl only interested in platonic relationships, any girl having a sense of vocation or a quality of leadership must automatically be a witch. 'I might almost . . . have been a man,' laments Joan towards the end of the play. 'Pity I wasn't; I should not have bothered you all so much then.'

For teenage girls it is perhaps hard to measure the success of the sexual revolution, but I like to hope that, standing unchaperoned at the stage door in Levi's and Doctor Marten boots, with their cropped hair-dos and their wonderful bubbling confidence as they poured forth their opinions and their aspirations, they got some measure of it.

As to Joan's relevance to me or mine to her – I'm not an intractable teenager, but I most certainly was once. I'm not a country girl, but I can see my Northumbrian origins as a source of reference. I'm not a lone girl amongst soldiers, but I was one of very few girls at a boys' school. I have not been drawn into conflict with every male authority figure I have encountered, but I have been in the first-year intake of women into a male college (Oxford's Exeter College) and I have witnessed the terror some men have of female intrusion into a male domain. I should also add that with our production, with male producers, a predominately male cast, and a female director, the opposite was true. Finally, like Joan, I think I am aware of the difference between 'Life' and 'Existence', and the potential destruction of all that seems to define 'Life' by cant and cynicism and misperception of reality. I have not heard voices – but I live in hope.

Whether she is considered miraculous or unbearable, the inspiration of women like Joan will always be relevant: 'O God, that madest this beautiful earth, when will it be ready to receive Thy saints? How long, O Lord, how long?'

All Joans are relevant but some Joans are more relevant than others – I think Shaw's Saint Joan is the right one to be received by the twenty-first century.

Introduction

by Joley Wood

In 1913, after already creating a significant body of work, George Bernard Shaw conceived of a drama about Joan of Arc in a letter to a friend. Shaw completed *Saint Joan* in 1923, and for the next two years the play encountered mixed reception (often in the same review), with criticisms of length and the epilogue often mitigated by acknowledgements of an underlying genius. In 1925 *Saint Joan* earned Shaw both his first success on the French stage and the Nobel Prize for Literature.

Saint Joan is Shaw's most acclaimed historically based play, what Thomas Mann called 'the most fervent thing Shaw ever wrote'. Luigi Pirandello felt that Shaw respected the 'considerations of art' and sustained a poetic emotion throughout the play. Shaw found in Joan's heresy a fitting emblem of the human spirit. In 1920 Joan of Arc was canonized a saint by the Catholic Church. Joan's brash yet accurate critique of authority resonated with Shaw, and he realized that her canonization risked whitewashing this most Shavian quality of hers. Shaw hoped that his play would restore this quality she had to the public eye, and modelled his Joan on friends of his who also challenged the social status quo: these included the physically vigorous, well-disciplined and seemingly sexless hostess of the Fabian Summer Schools, Mary Hankinson; and T. E. Lawrence, or Lawrence of Arabia, who had recently taken part in a Middle Eastern national unification movement similar to Joan's French endeavour. This kind of antagonistic character can be an enticing challenge for an actor to play, and since Sybil Thorndike many, including Joan Plowright, Frances de la Tour and, recently, Imogen Stubbs, have attempted to embody this spirit –

when a film version that was to be financed by General Charles de Gaulle was discussed, de Gaulle even suggested that he should play St Joan in preference to the casted Greta Garbo.

Shaw calls *Saint Joan* 'a Chronicle play', but it can be argued that he has written his own kind of tragedy, embodying a Shavian challenge to prevailing artistic and social norms. Artistically, Shaw challenges previously accepted models of stage tragedy by offering an alternative to the classical form. Aristotelian tragedy depends upon some flaw or error by the protagonist that sets the tragic machinery into motion. Shaw's notion of tragedy, however, functions on a different register. We are not invited to take part in someone's error, but in the distress one encounters when the right thing *was* done, yet failure was always imminent. Hence it is Joan's strengths, not her faults, that bring about her downfall. One critic has noted the similarity of Shaw's approach to tragedy and G. W. F. Hegel's outlook in his *Philosophy of Fine Art*: 'two opposed Rights come forth: the one breaks itself to pieces against the other: in this way, both alike suffer loss; while both alike are justified the one towards the other: not as if this were right, that other wrong'. Shaw's intentions seem like-minded. In his original Preface he notes 'It is what men do at their best, with good intentions, and what normal men and women find that they must and will do in spite of their intentions, that really concern us'; and Joan is burned 'by normally innocent people in the energy of their righteousness'. In other words, neither Joan nor her executioners are in error; both act with 'good' yet mutually contradictory intentions, the strain of which leads to the destruction of one or the other. Indeed, this may be a more poignant form of tragedy than one dealing in error. The audience of classical Aristotelian tragedy always has the consolation that the error leads to the downfall. Shaw removes this possibility by eliminating the error, sealing off those mental doors that offer some sense of relief, and thus brings his audience closer to a desperate tragic sense.

Aristotle was not the only Greek influence upon Shaw's tragedy. The narrative of Prometheus represented the 'staple of tragedy' for Shaw. The Titan gave fire to humanity against the wishes of the gods and was severely punished through eternal

physical torture, yet remained defiant and thus became a martyr
for his actions. Similarly, Joan gave nationhood to a people and
was then burned at the stake for being a heretical threat to the
authorities, yet still prayed while she burned – 'What more do
you want for a tragedy as great as that of Prometheus?' said
Shaw. In his original Preface to *Saint Joan*, Shaw also compared
Joan to Socrates: both had a similar ability to infuriate authorities because their actions had the side effect of revealing where
those authorities were wrong, or even foolish.

Shaw felt that this challenge of fresh principles to held ideals
was necessary for human evolution. Hence objections like
Joan's, pointing out where improvement is needed, may in many
cases be silenced, but history shows that such reactions only
prove the validity of the objection. Thus Prometheus' liver
becomes a scavenger's eternal lunch while he shows no remorse;
Socrates drinks his last tea while he continues teaching; and
Joan goes up in a blaze to her angels while she persists in praying
– all becoming martyrs for the cause of reason in the face of the
irrational. As Shaw wrote, 'the angels may weep at the murder,
but the gods laugh at the murderers'.

Shaw saw the irony of how Joan, after four long centuries,
was being brought into the fold of a suppressive authority she
stood against. Thus when she is canonized a saint in the
Epilogue, Shaw has Joan state 'But I never made any such claim.'
Joan's situation is ironically reflected in Shaw's winning the
Nobel Prize for the play. In its own way the Prize is a canonization of his spirit, yet it is hardly in keeping with the anti-
establishment tone of his drama: 'The Nobel Prize was a hideous
calamity for me,' he wrote to a friend; '. . . It was really almost
as bad as my 70th birthday.' Shaw had the final say by using
the award money to establish an Anglo-Swedish Literary
Foundation.

It is true that Shaw altered the historical facts somewhat in
his characterizations: this was not because his grasp on the facts
was loose, but rather to create the social tensions needed to
drive the play. He attempted to distil the facts of a historical
event in order to locate its sense and re-recreate that sense on
stage through an artistic means, a form that falls somewhere

between historiography and histrionics. Therefore, despite what history may show, no character in his play need be entirely good or bad – 'There are no villains in the piece,' Shaw wrote in his Preface, 'It is, I repeat, what normally innocent people do that concerns us.'

In effect Shaw creates a kind of absurdist social critique through his drama: the protagonist is sent into an irrational situation believed to be perfectly sound to everyone except her, and this situation is then logically followed to its irrational conclusion. Shaw shares this approach with other writers from his native Ireland, from Swift's social commentaries and Wilde's satires to Joyce's cultural observations and Beckett's existential critiques. 'English literature must be saved (by an Irishman, as usual),' wrote Shaw, 'from the disgrace of having nothing to show concerning Joan . . .'

The outsider who has found a way in often brings an unknown perspective to a culture, and this critique of the irrational is part of a tradition of analysis that does not simply turn things on its head, but shows how an ignored fault can eventually undo a greater structure. In this case Joan is the outsider to the established French Catholic Church and State. French Nationalism makes sense to Shaw's Joan, because it is she and other French-speaking peasants who require the attention of their king, not people who do not even live in France. Joan's desire to commune directly with her god without an overly bureaucratic clergy intervening reveals a Church that has unknowingly placed itself above the deity. And Joan's battle savvy and instincts were that of a soldier, so it was perfectly logical to her to be dressing and acting as such. This is a person achieving her potential, not a destiny determined by gender – and how would a 'womanly' woman be treated in a camp of soldiers? Not as a soldier. Joan did the commonsensical thing, and was persecuted for it. In a final Shavian twist, the Epilogue proves to the audience that, despite four centuries of hindsight, our mortal eyes would not be able to distinguish a saint from a heretic; were Joan alive today, she would still be persecuted.

SAINT JOAN

PREFACE

JOAN THE ORIGINAL
AND PRESUMPTUOUS

Joan of Arc, a village girl from the Vosges, was born about
1412; burnt for heresy, witchcraft, and sorcery in 1431; rehabilitated after a fashion in 1456; designated Venerable in 1904;
declared Blessed in 1908; and finally canonized in 1920. She is
the most notable Warrior Saint in the Christian calendar, and
the queerest fish among the eccentric worthies of the Middle
Ages. Though a professed and most pious Catholic, and the
projector of a Crusade against the Husites, she was in fact one
of the first Protestant martyrs. She was also one of the first
apostles of Nationalism, and the first French practitioner of
Napoleonic realism in warfare as distinguished from the sporting ransom-gambling chivalry of her time. She was the pioneer
of rational dressing for women, and, like Queen Christina of
Sweden two centuries later, to say nothing of Catalina de Erauso
and innumerable obscure heroines who have disguised themselves as men to serve as soldiers and sailors, she refused to
accept the specific woman's lot, and dressed and fought and
lived as men did.

As she contrived to assert herself in all these ways with such
force that she was famous throughout western Europe before
she was out of her teens (indeed she never got out of them), it is
hardly surprising that she was judicially burnt, ostensibly for a
number of capital crimes which we no longer punish as such,
but essentially for what we call unwomanly and insufferable

presumption. At eighteen Joan's pretensions were beyond those of the proudest Pope or the haughtiest emperor. She claimed to be the ambassador and plenipotentiary of God, and to be, in effect, a member of the Church Triumphant whilst still in the flesh on earth. She patronized her own king, and summoned the English king to repentance and obedience to her commands. She lectured, talked down, and overruled statesmen and prelates. She pooh-poohed the plans of generals, leading their troops to victory on plans of her own. She had an unbounded and quite unconcealed contempt for official opinion, judgment, and authority, and for War Office tactics and strategy. Had she been a sage and monarch in whom the most venerable hierarchy and the most illustrious dynasty converged, her pretensions and proceedings would have been as trying to the official mind as the pretensions of Caesar were to Cassius. As her actual condition was pure upstart, there were only two opinions about her. One was that she was miraculous: the other that she was unbearable.

JOAN AND SOCRATES

If Joan had been malicious, selfish, cowardly, or stupid, she would have been one of the most odious persons known to history instead of one of the most attractive. If she had been old enough to know the effect she was producing on the men whom she humiliated by being right when they were wrong, and had learned to flatter and manage them, she might have lived as long as Queen Elizabeth. But she was too young and rustical and inexperienced to have any such arts. When she was thwarted by men whom she thought fools, she made no secret of her opinion of them or her impatience with their folly; and she was naïve enough to expect them to be obliged to her for setting them right and keeping them out of mischief. Now it is always hard for superior wits to understand the fury roused by their exposures of the stupidities of comparative dullards. Even Socrates, for all his age and experience, did not defend himself at his trial like a man who understood the long accumulated fury that had burst on him, and was clamoring for his death. His accuser, if born 2300 years later, might have been picked out of any first class carriage on a suburban railway during the evening or morning rush from or to the City; for he had really nothing to say except that he and his like could not endure being shewn up as idiots every time Socrates opened his mouth. Socrates, unconscious of this, was paralyzed by his sense that somehow he was missing the point of the attack. He petered out after he had established the fact that he was an old soldier and a man of honorable life, and that his accuser was a silly snob. He had no suspicion of the extent to which his mental superiority had roused fear and hatred against him in the hearts of men towards whom he was conscious of nothing but good will and good service.

CONTRAST WITH NAPOLEON

If Socrates was as innocent as this at the age of seventy, it may be imagined how innocent Joan was at the age of seventeen. Now Socrates was a man of argument, operating slowly and peacefully on men's minds, whereas Joan was a woman of action, operating with impetuous violence on their bodies. That, no doubt, is why the contemporaries of Socrates endured him so long, and why Joan was destroyed before she was fully grown. But both of them combined terrifying ability with a frankness, personal modesty, and benevolence which made the furious dislike to which they fell victims absolutely unreasonable, and therefore inapprehensible by themselves. Napoleon, also possessed of terrifying ability, but neither frank nor disinterested, had no illusions as to the nature of his popularity. When he was asked how the world would take his death, he said it would give a gasp of relief. But it is not so easy for mental giants who neither hate nor intend to injure their fellows to realize that nevertheless their fellows hate mental giants and would like to destroy them, not only enviously because the juxtaposition of a superior wounds their vanity, but quite humbly and honestly because it frightens them. Fear will drive men to any extreme; and the fear inspired by a superior being is a mystery which cannot be reasoned away. Being immeasurable it is unbearable when there is no presumption or guarantee of its benevolence and moral responsibility: in other words, when it has no official status. The legal and conventional superiority of Herod and Pilate, and of Annas and Caiaphas, inspires fear; but the fear, being a reasonable fear of measurable and avoidable consequences which seem salutary and protective, is bearable; whilst the strange superiority of Christ and the fear it inspires elicit a shriek of Crucify Him from all who cannot divine its benevolence. Socrates has to drink the hemlock, Christ to hang on the cross, and Joan to burn at the stake, whilst Napoleon, though he ends in St Helena, at least dies in his bed there; and many terrifying but quite comprehensible official scoundrels die natural deaths in all the glory of the kingdoms of this world, proving that it is far more dangerous to be a saint than to be a conqueror. Those who have been both, like Mahomet and Joan, have found that it is the conqueror who must save the saint, and that defeat and capture mean martyrdom. Joan was burnt without a hand lifted on her own side to save her. The comrades she had led to victory and the enemies she had disgraced and defeated, the French king she had crowned and the English king whose crown she had kicked into the Loire, were equally glad to be rid of her.

WAS JOAN INNOCENT OR GUILTY?

As this result could have been produced by a crapulous inferiority as well as by a sublime superiority, the question which of the two was operative in Joan's case has to be faced. It was decided against her by her contemporaries after a very careful and conscientious trial; and the reversal of the verdict twenty-five years later, in form a rehabilitation of Joan, was really only a confirmation of the validity of the coronation of Charles VII. It is the more impressive reversal by a unanimous Posterity, culminating in her canonization, that has quashed the original proceedings, and put her judges on their trial, which, so far, has been much more unfair than their trial of her. Nevertheless the rehabilitation of 1456, corrupt job as it was, really did produce evidence enough to satisfy all reasonable critics that Joan was not a common termagant, not a harlot, not a witch, not a blasphemer, no more an idolater than the Pope himself, and not ill conducted in any sense apart from her soldiering, her wearing of men's clothes, and her audacity, but on the contrary good-humored, an intact virgin, very pious, very temperate (we should call her meal of bread soaked in the common wine which is the drinking water of France ascetic), very kindly, and, though a brave and hardy soldier, unable to endure loose language or licentious conduct. She went to the stake without a stain on her character except the overweening presumption, the superbity as they called it, that led her thither. It would therefore be waste of time now to prove that the Joan of the first part of the Elizabethan chronicle play of Henry VI (supposed to have been tinkered by Shakespear) grossly libels her in its concluding scenes in deference to Jingo patriotism. The mud that was thrown at her has dropped off by this time so completely that there is no need for any modern writer to wash up after it. What is far more difficult to get rid of is the mud that is being thrown at her judges, and the whitewash which disfigures her beyond recognition. When Jingo scurrility had done its worst to her, sectarian scurrility (in this case Protestant scurrility) used her stake to beat the Roman Catholic Church and the Inquisition. The easiest way to make these institutions the villains of a melodrama was to make The Maid its heroine. That melodrama may be dismissed as rubbish. Joan got a far fairer trial from the Church and the Inquisition than any prisoner of her type and in her situation gets nowadays in any official secular court; and the decision was strictly according to law. And she was not a melodramatic heroine: that is, a physically beautiful lovelorn parasite on an equally beautiful hero, but a genius and a saint, about as completely the opposite of a melodramatic heroine as it is possible for a human being to be.

Let us be clear about the meaning of the terms. A genius is a person who, seeing farther and probing deeper than other people, has a different set of ethical valuations from theirs, and has energy enough to give effect to this extra vision and its valuations in whatever manner best suits his or her specific talents. A saint is one who having practised heroic virtues, and enjoyed revelations or powers of the order which The Church classes technically as supernatural, is eligible for canonization. If a historian is an Anti-Feminist, and does not believe women to be capable of genius in the traditional masculine departments, he will never make anything of Joan, whose genius was turned to practical account mainly in soldiering and politics. If he is Rationalist enough to deny that saints exist, and to hold that new ideas cannot come otherwise than by conscious ratiocination, he will never catch Joan's likeness. Her ideal biographer must be free from nineteenth century prejudices and biases; must understand the Middle Ages, the Roman Catholic Church, and the Holy Roman Empire much more intimately than our Whig historians have ever understood them; and must be capable of throwing off sex partialities and their romance, and regarding woman as the female of the human species, and not as a different kind of animal with specific charms and specific imbecilities.

JOAN'S GOOD LOOKS

To put the last point roughly, any book about Joan which begins by describing her as a beauty may be at once classed as a romance. Not one of Joan's comrades, in village, court, or camp, even when they were straining themselves to please the king by praising her, ever claimed that she was pretty. All the men who alluded to the matter declared most emphatically that she was unattractive sexually to a degree that seemed to them miraculous, considering that she was in the bloom of youth, and neither ugly, awkward, deformed, nor unpleasant in her person. The evident truth is that like most women of her hardy managing type she seemed neutral in the conflict of sex because men were too much afraid of her to fall in love with her. She herself was not sexless: in spite of the virginity she had vowed up to a point, and preserved to her death, she never excluded the possibility of marriage for herself. But marriage, with its preliminary of the attraction, pursuit, and capture of a husband, was not her business: she had something else to do. Byron's formula, 'Man's love is of man's life a thing apart: 'tis woman's whole existence,' did not apply to her any more than to George Washington or any other masculine worker on the heroic scale. Had she lived in our time, picture postcards might have been sold of her as a general: they would not have been sold of her as a sultana. Nevertheless there is one reason for crediting her with a very remarkable face. A sculptor of her time in Orleans made a statue of a helmeted young woman with a face that is unique in art in point of being evidently not an ideal face but a portrait, and yet so uncommon as to be unlike any real woman one has ever seen. It is surmised that Joan served unconsciously as the sculptor's model. There is no proof of this; but those extraordinarily spaced eyes raise so powerfully the question 'If this woman be not Joan, who is she?' that I dispense with further evidence, and challenge those who disagree with me to prove a negative. It is a wonderful face, but quite neutral from the point of view of the operatic beauty fancier.

Such a fancier may perhaps be finally chilled by the prosaic fact that Joan was the defendant in a suit for breach of promise of marriage, and that she conducted her own case and won it.

JOAN'S SOCIAL POSITION

By class Joan was the daughter of a working farmer who was one of the headmen of his village, and transacted its feudal business for it with the neighbouring squires and their lawyers. When the castle in which the villagers were entitled to take refuge from raids became derelict, he organized a combination of half a dozen farmers to obtain possession of it so as to occupy it when there was any danger of invasion. As a child, Joan could please herself at times with being the young lady of this castle. Her mother and brothers were able to follow and share her fortune at court without making themselves notably ridiculous. These facts leave us no excuse for the popular romance that turns every heroine into either a princess or a beggarmaid. In the somewhat similar case of Shakespear a whole inverted

pyramid of wasted research has been based on the assumption
that he was an illiterate laborer, in the face of the plainest
evidence that his father was a man of business, and at one time
a very prosperous one, married to a woman of some social
pretensions. There is the same tendency to drive Joan into the
position of a hired shepherd girl, though a hired shepherd girl
in Domrémy would have deferred to her as the young lady of
the farm.

The difference between Joan's case and Shakespear's is that
Shakespear was not illiterate. He had been to school, and knew
as much Latin and Greek as most university passmen retain:
that is, for practical purposes, none at all. Joan was absolutely
illiterate. 'I do not know A from B' she said. But many princesses
at that time and for long after might have said the same. Marie
Antoinette, for instance, at Joan's age could not spell her own
name correctly. But this does not mean that Joan was an ignorant
person, or that she suffered from the diffidence and sense of
social disadvantage now felt by people who cannot read or
write. If she could not write letters, she could and did dictate
them and attach full and indeed excessive importance to them.
When she was called a shepherd lass to her face she very warmly
resented it, and challenged any woman to compete with her in
the household arts of the mistresses of well furnished houses.
She understood the political and military situation in France
much better than most of our newspaper fed university women-
graduates understand the corresponding situation of their own
country today. Her first convert was the neighboring comman-
dant at Vaucouleurs; and she converted him by telling him about
the defeat of the Dauphin's troops at the Battle of Herrings so
long before he had official news of it that he concluded she must
have had a divine revelation. This knowledge of and interest in
public affairs was nothing extraordinary among farmers in a
war-swept countryside. Politicians came to the door too often
sword in hand to be disregarded: Joan's people could not afford
to be ignorant of what was going on in the feudal world. They
were not rich; and Joan worked on the farm as her father did,
driving the sheep to pasture and so forth; but there is no evidence
or suggestion of sordid poverty, and no reason to believe that

Joan had to work as a hired servant works, or indeed to work at all when she preferred to go to confession, or dawdle about waiting for visions and listening to the church bells to hear voices in them. In short, much more of a young lady, and even of an intellectual, than most of the daughters of our petty bourgeoisie.

JOAN'S VOICES AND VISIONS

Joan's voices and visions have played many tricks with her reputation. They have been held to prove that she was mad, that she was a liar and impostor, that she was a sorceress (she was burned for this), and finally that she was a saint. They do not prove any of these things; but the variety of the conclusions reached shew how little our matter-of-fact historians know about other people's minds, or even about their own. There are people in the world whose imagination is so vivid that when they have an idea it comes to them as an audible voice, sometimes uttered by a visual figure. Criminal lunatic asylums are occupied largely by murderers who have obeyed voices. Thus a woman may hear voices telling her that she must cut her husband's throat and strangle her child as they lie asleep; and she may feel obliged to do what she is told. By a medico-legal superstition it is held in our courts that criminals whose temptations present themselves under these illusions are not responsible for their actions, and must be treated as insane. But the seers of visions and the hearers of revelations are not always criminals. The inspirations and intuitions and unconsciously reasoned conclusions of genius sometimes assume similar illusions. Socrates, Luther, Swedenborg, Blake saw visions and heard voices just as Saint Francis and Saint Joan did. If Newton's imagination had been of the same vividly dramatic kind he might have seen the ghost of Pythagoras walk into the orchard and explain why the apples were falling. Such an illusion would have invalidated neither the theory of gravitation nor Newton's general sanity. What is more, the visionary method of making the discovery would not be a whit more miraculous than the normal method.

The test of sanity is not the normality of the method but the reasonableness of the discovery. If Newton had been informed by Pythagoras that the moon was made of green cheese, then Newton would have been locked up. Gravitation, being a reasoned hypothesis which fitted remarkably well into the Copernican version of the observed physical facts of the universe, established Newton's reputation for extraordinary intelligence, and would have done so no matter how fantastically he had arrived at it. Yet his theory of gravitation is not so impressive a mental feat as his astounding chronology, which establishes him as the king of mental conjurors, but a Bedlamite king whose authority no one now accepts. On the subject of the eleventh horn of the beast seen by the prophet Daniel he was more fantastic than Joan, because his imagination was not dramatic but mathematical and therefore extraordinarily susceptible to numbers: indeed if all his works were lost except his chronology we should say that he was as mad as a hatter. As it is, who dares diagnose Newton as a madman?

In the same way Joan must be judged a sane woman in spite of her voices because they never gave her any advice that might not have come to her from her mother wit exactly as gravitation came to Newton. We can all see now, especially since the late war threw so many of our women into military life, that Joan's campaigning could not have been carried on in petticoats. This was not only because she did a man's work, but because it was morally necessary that sex should be left out of the question as between her and her comrades-in-arms. She gave this reason herself when she was pressed on the subject; and the fact that this entirely reasonable necessity came to her imagination first as an order from God delivered through the mouth of Saint Catherine does not prove that she was mad. The soundness of the order proves that she was unusually sane; but its form proves that her dramatic imagination played tricks with her senses. Her policy was also quite sound: nobody disputes that the relief of Orleans, followed up by the coronation at Rheims of the Dauphin as a counterblow to the suspicions then current of his legitimacy and consequently of his title, were military and political masterstrokes that saved France. They might have been planned by Napoleon or any other illusionproof genius. They came to Joan as an instruction from her Counsel, as she called her visionary saints; but she was none the less an able leader of men for imagining her ideas in this way.

THE EVOLUTIONARY APPETITE

What then is the modern view of Joan's voices and visions and messages from God? The nineteenth century said that they were delusions, but that as she was a pretty girl, and had been abominably ill-treated and finally done to death by a superstitious rabble of medieval priests hounded on by a corrupt political bishop, it must be assumed that she was the innocent dupe of these delusions. The twentieth century finds this explanation too vapidly commonplace, and demands something more mystic. I think the twentieth century is right, because an explanation which amounts to Joan being mentally defective instead of, as she obviously was, mentally excessive, will not wash. I cannot believe, nor, if I could, could I expect all my readers to believe, as Joan did, that three ocularly visible well dressed persons, named respectively Saint Catherine, Saint Margaret, and Saint Michael, came down from heaven and gave her certain instructions with which they were charged by God for her. Not that such a belief would be more improbable or fantastic than some modern beliefs which we all swallow; but there are fashions and family habits in belief, and it happens that, my fashion being Victorian and my family habit Protestant, I find myself unable to attach any such objective validity to the form of Joan's visions.

But that there are forces at work which use individuals for purposes far transcending the purpose of keeping these individuals alive and prosperous and respectable and safe and happy in the middle station in life, which is all any good bourgeois can reasonably require, is established by the fact that men will, in the pursuit of knowledge and of social readjustments for which they will not be a penny the better, and are indeed often many pence the worse, face poverty, infamy, exile, imprisonment,

dreadful hardship, and death. Even the selfish pursuit of personal power does not nerve men to the efforts and sacrifices
which are eagerly made in pursuit of extensions of our power
over nature, though these extensions may not touch the personal
life of the seeker at any point. There is no more mystery about
this appetite for knowledge and power than about the appetite
for food: both are known as facts and as facts only, the difference
between them being that the appetite for food is necessary to
the life of the hungry man and is therefore a personal appetite,
whereas the other is an appetite for evolution, and therefore a
superpersonal need.

The diverse manners in which our imaginations dramatize
the approach of the superpersonal forces is a problem for the
psychologist, not for the historian. Only, the historian must
understand that visionaries are neither impostors nor lunatics.
It is one thing to say that the figure Joan recognized as
St Catherine was not really St Catherine, but the dramatization
by Joan's imagination of that pressure upon her of the driving
force that is behind evolution which I have just called the evolutionary appetite. It is quite another to class her visions with the
vision of two moons seen by a drunken person, or with Brocken
spectres, echoes and the like. Saint Catherine's instructions were
far too cogent for that; and the simplest French peasant who
believes in apparitions of celestial personages to favored mortals
is nearer to the scientific truth about Joan than the Rationalist
and Materialist historians and essayists who feel obliged to set
down a girl who saw saints and heard them talking to her as
either crazy or mendacious. If Joan was mad, all Christendom
was mad too; for people who believe devoutly in the existence
of celestial personages are every whit as mad in that sense as the
people who think they see them. Luther, when he threw his
inkhorn at the devil, was no more mad than any other Augus-
tinian monk: he had a more vivid imagination, and had perhaps
eaten and slept less: that was all.

THE MERE ICONOGRAPHY DOES
NOT MATTER

All the popular religions in the world are made apprehensible by an array of legendary personages, with an Almighty Father, and sometimes a mother and divine child, as the central figures. These are presented to the mind's eye in childhood; and the result is a hallucination which persists strongly throughout life when it has been well impressed. Thus all the thinking of the hallucinated adult about the fountain of inspiration which is continually flowing in the universe, or about the promptings of virtue and the revulsions of shame: in short, about aspiration and conscience, both of which forces are matters of fact more obvious than electro-magnetism, is thinking in terms of the celestial vision. And when in the case of exceptionally imaginative persons, especially those practising certain appropriate austerities, the hallucination extends from the mind's eye to the body's, the visionary sees Krishna or the Buddha or the Blessed Virgin or St Catherine as the case may be.

THE MODERN EDUCATION
WHICH JOAN ESCAPED

It is important to everyone nowadays to understand this, because modern science is making short work of the hallucinations without regard to the vital importance of the things they symbolize. If Joan were reborn today she would be sent, first to a convent school in which she would be mildly taught to connect inspiration and conscience with St Catherine and St Michael exactly as she was in the fifteenth century, and then finished up with a very energetic training in the gospel of Saints Louis Pasteur and Paul Bert, who would tell her (possibly in visions but more probably in pamphlets) not to be a superstitious little fool, and to empty out St Catherine and the rest of the Catholic hagiology as an obsolete iconography of exploded myths. It would be rubbed into her that Galileo was a martyr, and his persecutors incorrigible ignoramuses, and that St Teresa's hormones had gone astray and left her incurably hyperpituitary or hyperadrenal or hysteroid or epileptoid or anything but asteroid. She would have been convinced by precept and experiment that baptism and receiving the body of her Lord were contemptible superstitions, and that vaccination and vivisection were enlightened practices. Behind her new Saints Louis and Paul there would be not only Science purifying Religion and being purified by it, but hypochondria, melancholia, cowardice, stupidity, cruelty, muckraking curiosity, knowledge without wisdom, and everything that the eternal soul in Nature loathes, instead of the virtues of which St Catherine was the figure head. As to the new rites, which would be the saner Joan? the one who carried little children to be baptized of water and the spirit, or the one who sent the police to force their parents to have the most villainous racial poison we know thrust into their veins? the one who told them the story of the angel and Mary, or the one who questioned them as to their experiences of the Edipus complex? the one to whom the consecrated wafer was the very body of the virtue that was her salvation, or the one who looked forward to a precise and convenient regulation of her health and her desires by a nicely calculated diet of thyroid extract, adrenalin, thymin, pituitrin, and insulin, with pick-me-ups of hormone stimulants, the blood being first carefully fortified with antibodies against all possible infections by inoculations of infected bacteria and serum from infected animals, and against old age by surgical extirpation of the reproductive ducts or weekly doses of monkey gland?

It is true that behind all these quackeries there is a certain body of genuine scientific physiology. But was there any the less a certain body of genuine psychology behind St Catherine and the Holy Ghost? And which is the healthier mind? the saintly mind or the monkey gland mind? Does not the present cry of Back to the Middle Ages, which has been incubating ever since the pre-Raphaelite movement began, mean that it is no longer our Academy pictures that are intolerable, but our credulities that have not the excuse of being superstitions, our cruelties that have not the excuse of barbarism, our persecutions that have not the excuse of religious faith, our shameless substitution of successful swindlers and scoundrels and quacks for saints as objects of worship, and our deafness and blindness to the calls and visions of the inexorable power that made us, and will destroy us if we disregard it? To Joan and her contemporaries we should appear as a drove of Gadarene swine, possessed by all the unclean spirits cast out by the faith and civilization of the Middle Ages, running violently down a steep place into a hell of high explosives. For us to set up our condition as a standard of sanity, and declare Joan mad because she never condescended to it, is to prove that we are not only lost but irredeemable. Let us then once for all drop all nonsense about Joan being cracked, and accept her as at least as sane as Florence Nightingale, who also combined a very simple iconography of religious belief with a mind so exceptionally powerful that it kept her in continual trouble with the medical and military panjandrums of her time.

FAILURES OF THE VOICES

That the voices and visions were illusory, and their wisdom all Joan's own, is shewn by the occasions on which they failed her, notably during her trial, when they assured her that she would be rescued. Here her hopes flattered her; but they were not unreasonable: her military colleague La Hire was in command of a considerable force not so very far off; and if the Armagnacs, as her party was called, had really wanted to rescue her, and had put anything like her own vigor into the enterprise, they could have attempted it with very fair chances of success. She did not understand that they were glad to be rid of her, nor that the rescue of a prisoner from the hands of the Church was a much more serious business for a medieval captain, or even a medieval king, than its mere physical difficulty as a military exploit suggested. According to her lights her expectation of a rescue was reasonable; therefore she heard Madame Saint Catherine assuring her it would happen, that being her way of finding out and making up her own mind. When it became

evident that she had miscalculated: when she was led to the
stake, and La Hire was not thundering at the gates of Rouen
nor charging Warwick's men-at-arms, she threw over Saint
Catherine at once, and recanted. Nothing could be more sane
or practical. It was not until she discovered that she had gained
nothing by her recantation but close imprisonment for life that
she withdrew it, and deliberately and explicitly chose burning
instead: a decision which shewed not only the extraordinary
decision of her character, but also a Rationalism carried to its
ultimate human test of suicide. Yet even in this the illusion
persisted; and she announced her relapse as dictated to her by
her voices.

JOAN A GALTONIC VISUALIZER

The most sceptical scientific reader may therefore accept as a
flat fact, carrying no implication of unsoundness of mind, that
Joan was what Francis Galton and other modern investigators of
human faculty call a visualizer. She saw imaginary saints just as
some other people see imaginary diagrams and landscapes with
numbers dotted about them, and are thereby able to perform
feats of memory and arithmetic impossible to non-visualizers.
Visualizers will understand this at once. Non-visualizers who
have never read Galton will be puzzled and incredulous. But a
very little inquiry among their acquaintances will reveal to them
that the mind's eye is more or less a magic lantern, and that the
street is full of normally sane people who have hallucinations
of all sorts which they believe to be part of the normal permanent
equipment of all human beings.

JOAN'S MANLINESS AND MILITARISM

Joan's other abnormality, too common among uncommon
things to be properly called a peculiarity, was her craze for
soldiering and the masculine life. Her father tried to frighten
her out of it by threatening to drown her if she ran away with

the soldiers, and ordering her brothers to drown her if he were not on the spot. This extravagance was clearly not serious: it must have been addressed to a child young enough to imagine that he was in earnest. Joan must therefore as a child have wanted to run away and be a soldier. The awful prospect of being thrown into the Meuse and drowned by a terrible father and her big brothers kept her quiet until the father had lost his terrors and the brothers yielded to her natural leadership; and by that time she had sense enough to know that the masculine and military life was not a mere matter of running away from home. But the taste for it never left her, and was fundamental in determining her career.

If anyone doubts this, let him ask himself why a maid charged with a special mission from heaven to the Dauphin (this was how Joan saw her very able plan for retrieving the desperate situation of the uncrowned king) should not have simply gone to the court as a maid, in woman's dress, and urged her counsel upon him in a woman's way, as other women with similar missions had come to his mad father and his wise grandfather. Why did she insist on having a soldier's dress and arms and sword and horse and equipment, and on treating her escort of soldiers as comrades, sleeping side by side with them on the floor at night as if there were no difference of sex between them? It may be answered that this was the safest way of travelling through a country infested with hostile troops and bands of marauding deserters from both sides. Such an answer has no weight because it applies to all the women who travelled in France at that time, and who never dreamt of travelling otherwise than as women. But even if we accept it, how does it account for the fact that when the danger was over, and she could present herself at court in feminine attire with perfect safety and obviously with greater propriety, she presented herself in her man's dress, and instead of urging Charles, like Queen Victoria urging the War Office to send Roberts to the Transvaal, to send D'Alençon, De Rais, La Hire and the rest to the relief of Dunois at Orleans, insisted that she must go herself and lead the assault in person? Why did she give exhibitions of her dexterity in handling a lance, and of her seat as a rider?

Why did she accept presents of armor and chargers and masculine surcoats, and in every action repudiate the conventional character of a woman? The simple answer to all these questions is that she was the sort of woman that wants to lead a man's life. They are to be found wherever there are armies on foot or navies on the seas, serving in male disguise, eluding detection for astonishingly long periods, and sometimes, no doubt, escaping it entirely. When they are in a position to defy public opinion they throw off all concealment. You have your Rosa Bonheur painting in male blouse and trousers, and George Sand living a man's life and almost compelling her Chopins and De Mussets to live women's lives to amuse her. Had Joan not been one of those 'unwomanly women', she might have been canonized much sooner.

But it is not necessary to wear trousers and smoke big cigars to live a man's life any more than it is necessary to wear petticoats to live a woman's. There are plenty of gowned and bodiced women in ordinary civil life who manage their own affairs and other people's, including those of their menfolk, and are entirely masculine in their tastes and pursuits. There always were such women, even in the Victorian days when women had fewer legal rights than men, and our modern women magistrates, mayors, and members of Parliament were unknown. In reactionary Russia in our own century a woman soldier organized an effective regiment of amazons, which disappeared only because it was Aldershottian enough to be against the Revolution. The exemption of women from military service is founded, not on any natural inaptitude that men do not share, but on the fact that communities cannot reproduce themselves without plenty of women. Men are more largely dispensable, and are sacrificed accordingly.

WAS JOAN SUICIDAL?

These two abnormalities were the only ones that were irresistibly prepotent in Joan; and they brought her to the stake. Neither of them was peculiar to her. There was nothing peculiar about her except the vigor and scope of her mind and character, and the intensity of her vital energy. She was accused of a suicidal tendency; and it is a fact that when she attempted to escape from Beaurevoir Castle by jumping from a tower said to be sixty feet high, she took a risk beyond reason, though she recovered from the crash after a few days fasting. Her death was deliberately chosen as an alternative to life without liberty. In battle she challenged death as Wellington did at Waterloo, and as Nelson habitually did when he walked his quarter deck during his battles with all his decorations in full blaze. As neither Nelson nor Wellington nor any of those who have performed desperate feats, and preferred death to captivity, has been accused of suicidal mania, Joan need not be suspected of it. In the Beaurevoir affair there was more at stake than her freedom. She was distracted by the news that Compiègne was about to fall; and she was convinced that she could save it if only she could get free. Still, the leap was so perilous that her conscience was not quite easy about it; and she expressed this, as usual, by saying that Saint Catherine had forbidden her to do it, but forgave her afterwards for her disobedience.

JOAN SUMMED UP

We may accept and admire Joan, then, as a sane and shrewd country girl of extraordinary strength of mind and hardihood of body. Everything she did was thoroughly calculated; and though the process was so rapid that she was hardly conscious of it, and ascribed it all to her voices, she was a woman of policy and not of blind impulse. In war she was as much a realist as Napoleon: she had his eye for artillery and his knowledge of what it could do. She did not expect besieged cities to fall Jerichowise at the sound of her trumpet, but, like Wellington, adapted her methods of attack to the peculiarities of the defence; and she anticipated the Napoleonic calculation that if you only hold on long enough the other fellow will give in: for example, her final triumph at Orleans was achieved after her commander Dunois had sounded the retreat at the end of a day's fighting without a decision. She was never for a moment what so many romancers and playwrights have pretended: a romantic young lady. She was a thorough daughter of the soil in her peasantlike matter-of-factness and doggedness, and her acceptance of great lords and kings and prelates as such without idolatry or snobbery, seeing at a glance how much they were individually good for. She had the respectable countrywoman's sense of the value of public decency, and would not tolerate foul language and neglect of religious observances, nor allow disreputable women to hang about her soldiers. She had one pious ejaculation 'En nom Dé!' and one meaningless oath 'Par mon martin'; and this much swearing she allowed to the incorrigibly blasphemous La Hire equally with herself. The value of this prudery was so great in restoring the self-respect of the badly demoralized army that, like most of her policy, it justified itself as soundly calculated. She talked to and dealt with people of all classes, from laborers to kings, without embarrassment or affectation, and got them to do what she wanted when they were not afraid or corrupt. She could coax and she could hustle, her tongue having a soft side and a sharp edge. She was very capable: a born boss.

JOAN'S IMMATURITY AND IGNORANCE

All this, however, must be taken with one heavy qualification. She was only a girl in her teens. If we could think of her as a managing woman of fifty we should seize her type at once; for we have plenty of managing women among us of that age who illustrate perfectly the sort of person she would have become had she lived. But she, being only a lass when all is said, lacked their knowledge of men's vanities and of the weight and proportion of social forces. She knew nothing of iron hands in velvet gloves: she just used her fists. She thought political changes much easier than they are, and, like Mahomet in his innocence of any world but the tribal world, wrote letters to kings calling on them to make millennial rearrangements. Consequently it was only in the enterprises that were really simple and compassable by swift physical force, like the coronation and the Orleans campaign, that she was successful.

Her want of academic education disabled her when she had
to deal with such elaborately artificial structures as the great
ecclesiastical and social institutions of the Middle Ages. She had
a horror of heretics without suspecting that she was herself a
heresiarch, one of the precursors of a schism that rent Europe
in two, and cost centuries of bloodshed that is not yet staunched.
She objected to foreigners on the sensible ground that they were
not in their proper place in France; but she had no notion
of how this brought her into conflict with Catholicism and
Feudalism, both essentially international. She worked by commonsense; and where scholarship was the only clue to institutions she was in the dark, and broke her shins against them,
all the more rudely because of her enormous self-confidence,
which made her the least cautious of human beings in civil
affairs.

This combination of inept youth and academic ignorance
with great natural capacity, push, courage, devotion, originality,
and oddity, fully accounts for all the facts in Joan's career, and
makes her a credible historical and human phenomenon; but it
clashes most discordantly both with the idolatrous romance
that has grown up around her, and the belittling scepticism that
reacts against that romance.

THE MAID IN LITERATURE

English readers would probably like to know how these idoliza-
tions and reactions have affected the books they are most
familiar with about Joan. There is the first part of the Shake-
spearean, or pseudo-Shakespearean trilogy of Henry VI, in
which Joan is one of the leading characters. This portrait of
Joan is not more authentic than the descriptions in the London
papers of George Washington in 1780, of Napoleon in 1803, of
the German Crown Prince in 1915, or of Lenin in 1917. It ends
in mere scurrility. The impression left by it is that the playwright,
having begun by an attempt to make Joan a beautiful and
romantic figure, was told by his scandalized company that English patriotism would never stand a sympathetic representation

of a French conqueror of English troops, and that unless he at
once introduced all the old charges against Joan of being a
sorceress and harlot, and assumed her to be guilty of all of them,
his play could not be produced. As likely as not, this is what
actually happened: indeed there is only one other apparent way
of accounting for the sympathetic representation of Joan as a
heroine culminating in her eloquent appeal to the Duke of
Burgundy, followed by the blackguardly scurrility of the concluding scenes. That other way is to assume that the original
play was wholly scurrilous, and that Shakespear touched up the
earlier scenes. As the work belongs to a period at which he was
only beginning his practice as a tinker of old works, before his
own style was fully formed and hardened, it is impossible to
verify this guess. His finger is not unmistakeably evident in the
play, which is poor and base in its moral tone; but he may
have tried to redeem it from down-right infamy by shedding a
momentary glamor on the figure of The Maid.

When we jump over two centuries to Schiller, we find Die
Jungfrau von Orleans drowned in a witch's caldron of raging
romance. Schiller's Joan has not a single point of contact with
the real Joan, nor indeed with any mortal woman that ever
walked this earth. There is really nothing to be said of his play
but that it is not about Joan at all, and can hardly be said to
pretend to be; for he makes her die on the battlefield, finding
her burning unbearable. Before Schiller came Voltaire, who
burlesqued Homer in a mock epic called La Pucelle. It is the
fashion to dismiss this with virtuous indignation as an obscene
libel; and I certainly cannot defend it against the charge of
extravagant indecorum. But its purpose was not to depict Joan,
but to kill with ridicule everything that Voltaire righteously
hated in the institutions and fashions of his own day. He made
Joan ridiculous, but not contemptible nor (comparatively)
unchaste; and as he also made Homer and St Peter and St Denis
and the brave Dunois ridiculous, and the other heroines of the
poem very unchaste indeed, he may be said to have let Joan off
very easily. But indeed the personal adventures of the characters
are so outrageous, and so Homerically free from any pretence
at or even possibility of historical veracity, that those who

affect to take them seriously only make themselves Pecksniffian. Samuel Butler believed The Iliad to be a burlesque of Greek Jingoism and Greek religion, written by a hostage or a slave; and La Pucelle makes Butler's theory almost convincing. Voltaire represents Agnes Sorel, the Dauphin's mistress, whom Joan never met, as a woman with a consuming passion for the chastest concubinal fidelity, whose fate it was to be continually falling into the hands of licentious foes and suffering the worst extremities of rapine. The combats in which Joan rides a flying donkey, or in which, taken unaware with no clothes on, she defends Agnes with her sword, and inflicts appropriate mutilations on her assailants, can be laughed at as they are intended to be without scruple; for no sane person could mistake them for sober history; and it may be that their ribald irreverence is more wholesome than the beglamored sentimentality of Schiller. Certainly Voltaire should not have asserted that Joan's father was a priest; but when he was out to *écraser l'infâme* (the French Church) he stuck at nothing.

So far, the literary representations of The Maid were legendary. But the publication by Quicherat in 1841 of the reports of her trial and rehabilitation placed the subject on a new footing. These entirely realistic documents created a living interest in Joan which Voltaire's mock Homerics and Schiller's romantic nonsense missed. Typical products of that interest in America and England are the histories of Joan by Mark Twain and Andrew Lang. Mark Twain was converted to downright worship of Joan directly by Quicherat. Later on, another man of genius, Anatole France, reacted against the Quicheratic wave of enthusiasm, and wrote a Life of Joan in which he attributed Joan's ideas to clerical prompting and her military success to an adroit use of her by Dunois as a *mascotte*: in short, he denied that she had any serious military or political ability. At this Andrew saw red, and went for Anatole's scalp in a rival Life of her which should be read as a corrective to the other. Lang had no difficulty in shewing that Joan's ability was not an unnatural fiction to be explained away as an illusion manufactured by priests and soldiers, but a straightforward fact.

It has been lightly pleaded in explanation that Anatole France is a Parisian of the art world, into whose scheme of things the able, hardheaded, hardhanded female, though she dominates provincial France and business Paris, does not enter; whereas Lang was a Scot, and every Scot knows that the grey mare is as likely as not to be the better horse. But this explanation does not convince me. I cannot believe that Anatole France does not know what everybody knows. I wish everybody knew all that he knows. One feels antipathies at work in his book. He is not anti-Joan; but he is anti-clerical, anti-mystic, and fundamentally unable to believe that there ever was any such person as the real Joan.

Mark Twain's Joan, skirted to the ground, and with as many petticoats as Noah's wife in a toy ark, is an attempt to combine Bayard with Esther Summerson from Bleak House into an unimpeachable American school teacher in armor. Like Esther Summerson she makes her creator ridiculous, and yet, being the work of a man of genius, remains a credible human goodygoody in spite of her creator's infatuation. It is the description rather than the valuation that is wrong. Andrew Lang and Mark Twain are equally determined to make Joan a beautiful and most ladylike Victorian; but both of them recognize and insist on her capacity for leadership, though the Scots scholar is less romantic about it than the Mississippi pilot. But then Lang was, by lifelong professional habit, a critic of biographies rather than a biographer, whereas Mark Twain writes his biography frankly in the form of a romance.

PROTESTANT MISUNDERSTANDINGS
OF THE MIDDLE AGES

They had, however, one disability in common. To understand Joan's history it is not enough to understand her character: you must understand her environment as well. Joan in a nineteenth–twentieth century environment is as incongruous a figure as she would appear were she to walk down Piccadilly today in her fifteenth century armor. To see her in her proper perspective you must understand Christendom and the Catholic Church, the Holy Roman Empire and the Feudal System, as they existed and were understood in the Middle Ages. If you confuse the Middle Ages with the Dark Ages, and are in the habit of ridiculing your aunt for wearing 'medieval clothes', meaning those in vogue in the eighteen-nineties, and are quite convinced that the world has progressed enormously, both morally and mechanically, since Joan's time, then you will never understand why Joan was burnt, much less feel that you might have voted for burning her yourself if you had been a member of the court that tried her; and until you feel that you know nothing essential about her.

That the Mississippi pilot should have broken down on this misunderstanding is natural enough. Mark Twain, the Innocent Abroad, who saw the lovely churches of the Middle Ages without a throb of emotion, author of A Yankee at the Court of King Arthur, in which the heroes and heroines of medieval chivalry are guys seen through the eyes of a street arab, was clearly out of court from the beginning. Andrew Lang was better read; but, like Walter Scott, he enjoyed medieval history as a string of Border romances rather than as the record of a high European civilization based on a catholic faith. Both of them were baptized as Protestants, and impressed by all their schooling and most of their reading with the belief that Catholic bishops who burnt heretics were persecutors capable of any villainy; that all heretics were Albigensians or Husites or Jews or Protestants of the highest character; and that the Inquisition was a Chamber of Horrors invented expressly and exclusively for such burnings. Accordingly we find them representing Peter Cauchon, Bishop of Beauvais, the judge who sent Joan to the stake, as an unconscionable scoundrel, and all the questions put to her as 'traps' to ensnare and destroy her. And they assume unhesitatingly that the two or three score of canons and doctors of law and divinity who sat with Cauchon as assessors, were exact reproductions of him on slightly less elevated chairs and with a different headdress.

COMPARATIVE FAIRNESS OF
JOAN'S TRIAL

The truth is that Cauchon was threatened and insulted by the
English for being too considerate to Joan. A recent French writer
denies that Joan was burnt, and holds that Cauchon spirited her
away and burnt somebody or something else in her place, and
that the pretender who subsequently personated her at Orleans
and elsewhere was not a pretender but the real authentic Joan.
He is able to cite Cauchon's pro-Joan partiality in support of
his view. As to the assessors, the objection to them is not that
they were a row of uniform rascals, but that they were political
partisans of Joan's enemies. This is a valid objection to all
such trials; but in the absence of neutral tribunals they are
unavoidable. A trial by Joan's French partisans would have been
as unfair as the trial by her French opponents; and an equally
mixed tribunal would have produced a deadlock. Such recent
trials as those of Edith Cavell by a German tribunal and Roger
Casement by an English one were open to the same objection;
but they went forward to the death nevertheless, because neutral
tribunals were not available. Edith, like Joan, was an arch
heretic: in the middle of the war she declared before the world
that 'Patriotism is not enough.' She nursed enemies back to
health, and assisted their prisoners to escape, making it abund-
antly clear that she would help any fugitive or distressed person
without asking whose side he was on, and acknowledging no
distinction before Christ between Tommy and Jerry and Pitou
the *poilu*. Well might Edith have wished that she could bring
the Middle Ages back, and have fifty civilians, learned in the
law or vowed to the service of God, to support two skilled
judges in trying her case according to the Catholic law of
Christendom, and to argue it out with her at sitting after sitting
for many weeks. The modern military Inquisition was not so
squeamish. It shot her out of hand; and her countrymen, seeing
in this a good opportunity for lecturing the enemy on his intolerance, put up a statue to her, but took particular care not to

inscribe on the pedestal 'Patriotism is not enough', for which omission, and the lie it implies, they will need Edith's intercession when they are themselves brought to judgment, if any heavenly power thinks such moral cowards capable of pleading to an intelligible indictment.

The point need be no further labored. Joan was persecuted essentially as she would be persecuted today. The change from burning to hanging or shooting may strike us as a change for the better. The change from careful trial under ordinary law to recklessly summary military terrorism may strike us as a change for the worse. But as far as toleration is concerned the trial and execution in Rouen in 1431 might have been an event of today; and we may charge our consciences accordingly. If Joan had to be dealt with by us in London she would be treated with no more toleration than Miss Sylvia Pankhurst, or the Peculiar People, or the parents who keep their children from the elementary school, or any of the others who cross the line we have to draw, rightly or wrongly, between the tolerable and the intolerable.

JOAN NOT TRIED AS A POLITICAL OFFENDER

Besides, Joan's trial was not, like Casement's, a national political trial. Ecclesiastical courts and the courts of the Inquisition (Joan was tried by a combination of the two) were Courts Christian: that is, international courts; and she was tried, not as a traitress, but as a heretic, blasphemer, sorceress, and idolater. Her alleged offences were not political offences against England, nor against the Burgundian faction in France, but against God and against the common morality of Christendom. And although the idea we call Nationalism was so foreign to the medieval conception of Christian society that it might almost have been directly charged against Joan as an additional heresy, yet it was not so charged; and it is unreasonable to suppose that the political bias of a body of Frenchmen like the assessors would on this point have run strongly in favor of the English foreigners (even if they had been making themselves particularly agreeable in France instead of just the contrary) against a Frenchwoman who had vanquished them.

The tragic part of the trial was that Joan, like most prisoners tried for anything but the simplest breaches of the ten commandments, did not understand what they were accusing her of. She was much more like Mark Twain than like Peter Cauchon. Her attachment to the Church was very different from the Bishop's, and does not, in fact, bear close examination from his point of view. She delighted in the solaces the Church offers to sensitive souls: to her, confession and communion were luxuries beside which the vulgar pleasures of the senses were trash. Her prayers were wonderful conversations with her three saints. Her piety seemed superhuman to the formally dutiful people whose religion was only a task to them. But when the Church was not offering her her favorite luxuries, but calling on her to accept its interpretation of God's will, and to sacrifice her own, she flatly refused, and made it clear that her notion of a Catholic Church was one in which the Pope was Pope Joan. How could the Church tolerate that, when it had just destroyed Hus, and had watched the career of Wycliffe with a growing anger that would have brought him, too, to the stake, had he not died a natural death before the wrath fell on him in his grave? Neither Hus nor Wycliffe was as bluntly defiant as Joan: both were reformers of the Church like Luther; whilst Joan, like Mrs Eddy, was quite prepared to supersede St Peter as the rock on which the Church was built, and, like Mahomet, was always ready with a private revelation from God to settle every question and fit every occasion.

The enormity of Joan's pretension was proved by her own unconsciousness of it, which we call her innocence, and her friends called her simplicity. Her solutions of the problems presented to her seemed, and indeed mostly were, the plainest commonsense, and their revelation to her by her Voices was to her a simple matter of fact. How could plain commonsense and simple fact seem to her to be that hideous thing, heresy? When rival prophetesses came into the field, she was down on them at once for liars and humbugs; but she never thought of them as heretics. She was in a state of invincible ignorance as to the Church's view; and the Church could not tolerate her pretensions without either waiving its authority or giving her a place beside the Trinity during her lifetime and in her teens, which was unthinkable. Thus an irresistible force met an immovable obstacle, and developed the heat that consumed poor Joan.

Mark and Andrew would have shared her innocence and her fate had they been dealt with by the Inquisition: that is why their accounts of the trial are as absurd as hers might have been could she have written one. All that can be said for their assumption that Cauchon was a vulgar villain, and that the questions put to Joan were traps, is that it has the support of the inquiry which rehabilitated her twenty-five years later. But this rehabilitation was as corrupt as the contrary proceeding applied to Cromwell by our Restoration reactionaries. Cauchon had been dug up, and his body thrown into the common sewer. Nothing was easier than to accuse him of cozenage, and declare the whole trial void on that account. That was what everybody wanted, from Charles the Victorious, whose credit was bound up with The Maid's, to the patriotic Nationalist populace, who idolized Joan's memory. The English were gone; and a verdict in their favour would have been an outrage on the throne and on the patriotism which Joan had set on foot.

We have none of these overwhelming motives of political convenience and popularity to bias us. For us the first trial stands valid; and the rehabilitation would be negligible but for the mass of sincere testimony it produced as to Joan's engaging personal character. The question then arises: how did The Church get over the verdict at the first trial when it canonized Joan five hundred years later?

THE CHURCH UNCOMPROMISED
BY ITS AMENDS

Easily enough. In the Catholic Church, far more than in law, there is no wrong without a remedy. It does not defer to Joanesque private judgment as such, the supremacy of private judgment for the individual being the quintessence of Protestantism; nevertheless it finds a place for private judgment *in excelsis* by admitting that the highest wisdom may come as a divine revelation to an individual. On sufficient evidence it will declare that individual a saint. Thus, as revelation may come by way of an enlightenment of the private judgment no less than by the words of a celestial personage appearing in a vision, a saint may be defined as a person of heroic virtue whose private judgment is privileged. Many innovating saints, notably Francis and Clare, have been in conflict with the Church during their lives, and have thus raised the question whether they were heretics or saints. Francis might have gone to the stake had he lived longer. It is therefore by no means impossible for a person to be excommunicated as a heretic, and on further consideration canonized as a saint. Excommunication by a provincial ecclesiastical court is not one of the acts for which the Church claims infallibility. Perhaps I had better inform my Protestant readers that the famous Dogma of Papal Infallibility is by far the most modest pretension of the kind in existence. Compared with our infallible democracies, our infallible medical councils, our infallible astronomers, our infallible judges, and our infallible parliaments, the Pope is on his knees in the dust confessing his ignorance before the throne of God, asking only that as to certain historical matters on which he has clearly more sources of information open to him than anyone else his decision shall be taken as final. The Church may, and perhaps some day will, canonize Galileo without compromising such infallibility as it claims for the Pope, if not without compromising the infallibility claimed for the Book of Joshua by simple souls whose rational faith in more important things has become bound up with a quite irrational faith in the chronicle of Joshua's campaigns as a treatise on physics. Therefore the Church will probably not canonize Galileo yet awhile, though it might do worse. But it has been able to canonize Joan without any compromise at all. She never doubted that the sun went round the earth: she had seen it do so too often.

Still, there was a great wrong done to Joan and to the conscience of the world by her burning. *Tout comprendre, c'est tout pardonner*, which is the Devil's sentimentality, cannot excuse it. When we have admitted that the tribunal was not only honest and legal, but exceptionally merciful in respect of sparing Joan the torture which was customary when she was obdurate as to taking the oath, and that Cauchon was far more self-disciplined and conscientious both as priest and lawyer than any English judge ever dreams of being in a political case in which his party and class prejudices are involved, the human fact remains that the burning of Joan of Arc was a horror, and that a historian who would defend it would defend anything. The final criticism of its physical side is implied in the refusal of the Marquesas islanders to be persuaded that the English did not eat Joan. Why, they ask, should anyone take the trouble to roast a human being except with that object? They cannot conceive its being a pleasure. As we have no answer for them that is not shameful to us, let us blush for our more complicated and pretentious savagery before we proceed to unravel the business further, and see what other lessons it contains for us.

CRUELTY, MODERN AND MEDIEVAL

First, let us get rid of the notion that the mere physical cruelty of the burning has any special significance. Joan was burnt just as dozens of less interesting heretics were burnt in her time. Christ, in being crucified, only shared the fate of thousands of forgotten malefactors. They have no pre-eminence in mere physical pain: much more horrible executions than theirs are on record, to say nothing of the agonies of so-called natural death at its worst.

Joan was burnt more than five hundred years ago. More than three hundred years later: that is, only about a hundred years before I was born, a woman was burnt on Stephen's Green in my native city of Dublin for coining, which was held to be treason. In my preface to the recent volume on English Prisons under Local Government, by Sidney and Beatrice Webb, I have mentioned that when I was already a grown man I saw Richard Wagner conduct two concerts, and that when Richard Wagner was a young man he saw and avoided a crowd of people hastening to see a soldier broken on the wheel by the more cruel of the two ways of carrying out that hideous method of execution. Also that the penalty of hanging, drawing, and quartering, unmentionable in its details, was abolished so recently that there are men living who have been sentenced to it. We are still flogging criminals, and clamoring for more flogging. Not even the most sensationally frightful of these atrocities inflicted on its victim the misery, degradation, and conscious waste and loss of life suffered in our modern prisons, especially the model ones, without, as far as I can see, rousing any more compunction than the burning of heretics did in the Middle Ages. We have not even the excuse of getting some fun out of our prisons as the Middle Ages did out of their stakes and wheels and gibbets. Joan herself judged this matter when she had to choose between imprisonment and the stake, and chose the stake. And thereby she deprived The Church of the plea that it was guiltless of her death, which was the work of the secular arm. The Church should have confined itself to excommunicating her. There it was within its rights: she had refused to accept its authority or comply with its conditions; and it could say with truth 'You are not one of us: go forth and find the religion that suits you, or found one for yourself.' It had no right to say 'You may return to us now that you have recanted; but you shall stay in a dungeon all the rest of your life.' Unfortunately, The Church did not believe that there was any genuine soul saving religion outside itself; and it was deeply corrupted, as all the Churches were and still are, by primitive Calibanism (in Browning's sense), or the propitiation of a dreaded deity by suffering and sacrifice. Its method was not cruelty for cruelty's sake, but cruelty for the salvation of Joan's soul. Joan, however, believed that the saving of her soul was her own business, and not that of *les gens d'église*. By using that term as she did, mistrustfully and contemptuously, she announced herself as, in germ, an anti-Clerical as thoroughgoing as Voltaire or Anatole France. Had she said in so many words 'To the dustbin with the Church Militant and its blackcoated officials: I recognize only the Church Triumphant in heaven,' she would hardly have put her view more plainly.

CATHOLIC ANTI-CLERICALISM

I must not leave it to be inferred here that one cannot be an anti-Clerical and a good Catholic too. All the reforming Popes have been vehement anti-Clericals, veritable scourges of the clergy. All the great Orders arose from dissatisfaction with the priests: that of the Franciscans with priestly snobbery, that of the Dominicans with priestly laziness and Laodiceanism, that of the Jesuits with priestly apathy and ignorance and indiscipline. The most bigoted Ulster Orangeman or Leicester Low Church bourgeois (as described by Mr Henry Nevinson) is a mere Gallio compared to Machiavelli, who, though no Protestant, was a fierce anti-Clerical. Any Catholic may, and many Catholics do, denounce any priest or body of priests, as lazy, drunken, idle, dissolute, and unworthy of their great Church and their function as the pastors of their flocks of human souls. But to say that the souls of the people are no business of the Churchmen is to go a step further, a step across the Rubicon. Joan virtually took that step.

CATHOLICISM NOT YET
CATHOLIC ENOUGH

And so, if we admit, as we must, that the burning of Joan was a mistake, we must broaden Catholicism sufficiently to include her in its charter. Our Churches must admit that no official organization of mortal men whose vocation does not carry with it extraordinary mental powers (and this is all that any Church Militant can in the face of fact and history pretend to be), can keep pace with the private judgment of persons of genius except when, by a very rare accident, the genius happens to be Pope, and not even then unless he is an exceedingly overbearing Pope. The Churches must learn humility as well as teach it. The Apostolic Succession cannot be secured or confined by the laying on of hands: the tongues of fire have descended on heathens and outcasts too often for that, leaving anointed Churchmen to scandalize History as worldly rascals. When the Church Militant behaves as if it were already the Church Triumphant, it makes these appalling blunders about Joan and Bruno and Galileo and the rest which make it so difficult for a Freethinker to join it; and a Church which has no place for Free-thinkers: nay, which does not inculcate and encourage freethinking with a complete belief that thought, when really free, must by its own law take the path that leads to The Church's bosom, not only has no future in modern culture, but obviously has no faith in the valid science of its own tenets, and is guilty of the heresy that theology and science are two different and opposite impulses, rivals for human allegiance.

I have before me the letter of a Catholic priest. 'In your play,' he writes, 'I see the dramatic presentation of the conflict of the Regal, sacerdotal, and Prophetical powers, in which Joan was crushed. To me it is not the victory of any one of them over the others that will bring peace and the Reign of the Saints in the Kingdom of God, but their fruitful interaction in a costly but noble state of tension.' The Pope himself could not put it better; nor can I. We must accept the tension, and maintain it nobly without letting ourselves be tempted to relieve it by burning the thread. This is Joan's lesson to The Church; and its formulation by the hand of a priest emboldens me to claim that her canonization was a magnificently Catholic gesture as the canonization of a Protestant saint by the Church of Rome. But its special value and virtue cannot be apparent until it is known and understood as such. If any simple priest for whom this is too hard a saying tells me that it was not so intended, I shall remind him that the Church is in the hands of God, and not, as simple priests imagine, God in the hands of the Church; so if he answers too confidently for God's intentions he may be asked 'Hast thou entered into the springs of the sea? or hast thou walked in the recesses of the deep?' And Joan's own answer is also the answer of old: 'Though He slay me, yet will I trust in Him; *but I will maintain my own ways before Him.*'

THE LAW OF CHANGE IS THE
LAW OF GOD

When Joan maintained her own ways she claimed, like Job, that there was not only God and the Church to be considered, but the Word made Flesh: that is, the unaveraged individual, representing life possibly at its highest actual human evolution and possibly at its lowest, but never at its merely mathematical average. Now there is no deification of the democratic average in the theory of the Church: it is an avowed hierarchy in which the members are sifted until at the end of the process an individual stands supreme as the Vicar of Christ. But when the process is examined it appears that its successive steps of selection and election are of the superior by the inferior (the cardinal vice of democracy), with the result that great popes are as rare and accidental as great kings, and that it has sometimes been safer for an aspirant to the Chair and the Keys to pass as a moribund dotard than as an energetic saint. At best very few popes have been canonized, or could be without letting down the standard of sanctity set by the self-elected saints.

No other result could have been reasonably expected; for it is not possible that an official organization of the spiritual needs of millions of men and women, mostly poor and ignorant, should compete successfully in the selection of its principals with the direct choice of the Holy Ghost as it flashes with unerring aim upon the individual. Nor can any College of Cardinals pray effectively that its choice may be inspired. The conscious prayer of the inferior may be that his choice may light on a greater than himself; but the sub-conscious intention of his self-preserving individuality must be to find a trustworthy servant for his own purposes. The saints and prophets, though they may be accidentally in this or that official position or rank, are always really self-selected, like Joan. And since neither Church nor State, by the secular necessities of its constitution, can guarantee even the recognition of such self-chosen missions, there is nothing for us but to make it a point of honor to privilege heresy to the last bearable degree on the simple ground that all evolution in thought and conduct must at first appear as heresy and misconduct. In short, though all society is founded on intolerance, all improvement is founded on tolerance, or the recognition of the fact that the law of evolution is Ibsen's law of change. And as the law of God in any sense of the word which can now command a faith proof against science is a law of evolution, it follows that the law of God is a law of change, and that when the Churches set themselves against change as such, they are setting themselves against the law of God.

CREDULITY, MODERN AND MEDIEVAL

When Abernethy, the famous doctor, was asked why he indulged himself with all the habits he warned his patients against as unhealthy, he replied that his business was that of a direction post, which points out the way to a place, but does not go thither itself. He might have added that neither does it compel the traveller to go thither, nor prevent him from seeking some other way. Unfortunately our clerical direction posts always do coerce the traveller when they have the political power to do so. When the Church was a temporal as well as a spiritual power, and for long after to the full extent to which it could control or influence the temporal power, it enforced conformity by persecutions that were all the more ruthless because their intention was so excellent. Today, when the doctor has succeeded to the priest, and can do practically what he likes with parliament and the press through the blind faith in him which has succeeded to the far more critical faith in the parson, legal compulsion to take the doctor's prescription, however poisonous, is carried to an extent that would have horrified the Inquisition and staggered Archbishop Laud. Our credulity is grosser than that of the Middle Ages, because the priest had no such direct pecuniary interest in our sins as the doctor has in our diseases: he did not starve when all was well with his flock, nor prosper when they were perishing, as our private commercial doctors must. Also the medieval cleric believed that something extremely unpleasant would happen to him after death if he was unscrupulous, a belief now practically extinct among persons receiving a dogmatically materialist education. Our professional corporations are Trade Unions without souls to be damned; and they will soon drive us to remind them that they have bodies to be kicked. The Vatican was never soulless: at worst it was a political conspiracy to make the Church supreme temporally as well as spiritually. Therefore the question raised by Joan's burning is a burning question still, though the penalties involved are not so sensational. That is why I am probing it. If it were only an historical curiosity I would not waste my readers' time and my own on it for five minutes.

TOLERATION, MODERN AND MEDIEVAL

The more closely we grapple with it the more difficult it becomes. At first sight we are disposed to repeat that Joan should have been excommunicated and then left to go her own way, though she would have protested vehemently against so cruel a deprivation of her spiritual food: for confession, absolution, and the body of her Lord were first necessaries of life to her. Such a spirit as Joan's might have got over that difficulty as the Church of England got over the Bulls of Pope Leo, by making a Church of her own, and affirming it to be the temple of the true and original faith from which her persecutors had strayed. But as such a proceeding was, in the eyes of both Church and State at that time, a spreading of damnation and anarchy, its toleration involved a greater strain on faith in freedom than political and ecclesiastical human nature could bear. It is easy to say that the Church should have waited for the alleged evil results instead of assuming that they would occur, and what they would be. That sounds simple enough; but if a modern Public Health Authority were to leave people entirely to their own devices in the matter of sanitation, saying, 'We have nothing to do with drainage or your views about drainage; but if you catch smallpox or typhus we will prosecute you and have you punished very severely like the authorities in Butler's Erewhon,' it would either be removed to the County Asylum or reminded that A's neglect of sanitation may kill the child of B two miles off, or start an epidemic in which the most conscientious sanitarians may perish.

We must face the fact that society is founded on intolerance. There are glaring cases of the abuse of intolerance; but they are quite as characteristic of our own age as of the Middle Ages. The typical modern example and contrast is compulsory inoculation replacing what was virtually compulsory baptism. But compulsion to inoculate is objected to as a crudely unscientific and mischievous anti-sanitary quackery, not in the least because we think it wrong to compel people to protect their children from disease. Its opponents would make it a crime, and will probably succeed in doing so; and that will be just as intolerant as making it compulsory. Neither the Pasteurians nor their opponents the Sanitarians would leave parents free to bring up their children naked, though that course also has some plausible advocates. We may prate of toleration as we will; but society must always draw a line somewhere between allowable conduct and insanity or crime, in spite of the risk of mistaking sages for lunatics and saviors for blasphemers. We must persecute, even to the death; and all we can do to mitigate the danger of persecution is, first, to

be very careful what we persecute, and second, to bear in mind
that unless there is a large liberty to shock conventional people,
and a well informed sense of the value of originality, individuality, and eccentricity, the result will be apparent stagnation
covering a repression of evolutionary forces which will eventually
explode with extravagant and probably destructive violence.

VARIABILITY OF TOLERATION

The degree of tolerance attainable at any moment depends on
the strain under which society is maintaining its cohesion. In
war, for instance, we suppress the gospels and put Quakers in
prison, muzzle the newspapers, and make it a serious offence to
shew a light at night. Under the strain of invasion the French
Government in 1792 struck off 4000 heads, mostly on grounds
that would not in time of settled peace have provoked any
Government to chloroform a dog; and in 1920 the British
Government slaughtered and burnt in Ireland to persecute the
advocates of a constitutional change which it had presently to
effect itself. Later on the Fascisti in Italy did everything that the
Black and Tans did in Ireland, with some grotesquely ferocious
variations, under the strain of an unskilled attempt at industrial
revolution by Socialists who understood Socialism even less
than Capitalists understand Capitalism. In the United States an
incredibly savage persecution of Russians took place during the
scare spread by the Russian Bolshevik revolution after 1917.
These instances could easily be multiplied; but they are enough
to shew that between a maximum of indulgent toleration and a
ruthlessly intolerant Terrorism there is a scale through which
toleration is continually rising or falling, and that there was not
the smallest ground for the self-complacent conviction of the
nineteenth century that it was more tolerant than the fifteenth,
or that such an event as the execution of Joan could not possibly occur in what we call our own more enlightened times.
Thousands of women, each of them a thousand times less
dangerous and terrifying to our Governments than Joan was to
the Government of her day, have within the last ten years been

slaughtered, starved to death, burnt out of house and home, and what not that Persecution and Terror could do to them, in the course of Crusades far more tyrannically pretentious than the medieval Crusades which proposed nothing more hyperbolical than the rescue of the Holy Sepulchre from the Saracens. The Inquisition, with its English equivalent the Star Chamber, are gone in the sense that their names are now disused; but can any of the modern substitutes for the Inquisition, the Special Tribunals and Commissions, the punitive expeditions, the suspensions of the Habeas Corpus Act, the proclamations of martial law and of minor states of siege, and the rest of them, claim that their victims have as fair a trial, as well considered a body of law to govern their cases, or as conscientious a judge to insist on strict legality of procedure as Joan had from the Inquisition and from the spirit of the Middle Ages even when her country was under the heaviest strain of civil and foreign war? From us she would have had no trial and no law except a Defence of The Realm Act suspending all law; and for judge she would have had, at best, a bothered major, and at worst a promoted advocate in ermine and scarlet to whom the scruples of a trained ecclesiastic like Cauchon would seem ridiculous and ungentlemanly.

THE CONFLICT BETWEEN GENIUS
AND DISCIPLINE

Having thus brought the matter home to ourselves, we may now consider the special feature of Joan's mental constitution which made her so unmanageable. What is to be done on the one hand with rulers who will not give any reason for their orders, and on the other with people who cannot understand the reasons when they are given? The government of the world, political, industrial, and domestic, has to be carried on mostly by the giving and obeying of orders under just these conditions. 'Dont argue: do as you are told' has to be said not only to children and soldiers, but practically to everybody. Fortunately most people do not want to argue: they are only too glad to be saved the trouble of thinking for themselves. And the ablest and most independent thinkers are content to understand their own special department. In other departments they will unhesitatingly ask for and accept the instructions of a policeman or the advice of a tailor without demanding or desiring explanations.

Nevertheless, there must be some ground for attaching authority to an order. A child will obey its parents, a soldier his officer, a philosopher a railway porter, and a workman a foreman, all without question, because it is generally accepted that those who give the orders understand what they are about, and are duly authorized and even obliged to give them, and because, in the practical emergencies of daily life, there is no time for lessons and explanations, or for arguments as to their validity. Such obediences are as necessary to the continuous operation of our social system as the revolutions of the earth are to the succession of night and day. But they are not so spontaneous as they seem: they have to be very carefully arranged and maintained. A bishop will defer to and obey a king; but let a curate venture to give him an order, however necessary and sensible, and the bishop will forget his cloth and damn the curate's impudence. The more obedient a man is to accredited authority the more jealous he is of allowing any unauthorized person to order him about.

With all this in mind, consider the career of Joan. She was a village girl, in authority over sheep and pigs, dogs and chickens, and to some extent over her father's hired laborers when he hired any, but over no one else on earth. Outside the farm she had no authority, no prestige, no claim to the smallest deference. Yet she ordered everybody about, from her uncle to the king, the archbishop, and the military General Staff. Her uncle obeyed her like a sheep, and took her to the castle of the local commander, who, on being ordered about, tried to assert himself, but soon collapsed and obeyed. And so on up to the king, as we have seen. This would have been unbearably irritating even if her orders had been offered as rational solutions of the desperate difficulties in which her social superiors found themselves just then. But they were not so offered. Nor were they offered as the expression of Joan's arbitrary will. It was never 'I say so,' but always 'God says so.'

JOAN AS THEOCRAT

Leaders who take that line have no trouble with some people, and no end of trouble with others. They need never fear a lukewarm reception. Either they are messengers of God, or they are blasphemous impostors. In the Middle Ages the general belief in witchcraft greatly intensified this contrast, because when an apparent miracle happened (as in the case of the wind changing at Orleans) it proved the divine mission to the credulous, and proved a contract with the devil to the sceptical. All through, Joan had to depend on those who accepted her as an incarnate angel against those who added to an intense resentment of her presumption a bigoted abhorrence of her as a witch. To this abhorrence we must add the extreme irritation of those who did not believe in the voices, and regarded her as a liar and impostor. It is hard to conceive anything more infuriating to a statesman or a military commander, or to a court favorite, than to be overruled at every turn, or to be robbed of the ear of the reigning sovereign, by an impudent young upstart practising on the credulity of the populace and the vanity and silliness of an immature prince by exploiting a few of those lucky coincidences which pass as miracles with uncritical people. Not only were the envy, snobbery, and competitive ambition of the baser natures exacerbated by Joan's success, but among the friendly ones that were clever enough to be critical a quite reasonable scepticism and mistrust of her ability, founded on a fair observation of her obvious ignorance and temerity, were at work against her. And as she met all remonstrances and all criticisms, not with arguments or persuasion, but with a flat appeal to the authority of God and a claim to be in God's special confidence, she must have seemed, to all who were not infatuated by her, so insufferable that nothing but an unbroken chain of overwhelming successes in the military and political field could have saved her from the wrath that finally destroyed her.

UNBROKEN SUCCESS ESSENTIAL
IN THEOCRACY

To forge such a chain she needed to be the King, the Archbishop of Rheims, the Bastard of Orleans, and herself into the bargain; and that was impossible. From the moment when she failed to stimulate Charles to follow up his coronation with a swoop on Paris she was lost. The fact that she insisted on this whilst the king and the rest timidly and foolishly thought they could square the Duke of Burgundy, and effect a combination with him against the English, made her a terrifying nuisance to them; and from that time onward she could do nothing but prowl about the battlefields waiting for some lucky chance to sweep the captains into a big move. But it was to the enemy that the chance came: she was taken prisoner by the Burgundians fighting before Compiègne, and at once discovered that she had not a friend in the political world. Had she escaped she would probably have fought on until the English were gone, and then had to shake the dust of the court off her feet, and retire to Domrémy as Garibaldi had to retire to Caprera.

MODERN DISTORTIONS OF
JOAN'S HISTORY

This, I think, is all that we can now pretend to say about the prose of Joan's career. The romance of her rise, the tragedy of her execution, and the comedy of the attempts of posterity to make amends for that execution, belong to my play and not to my preface, which must be confined to a sober essay on the facts. That such an essay is badly needed can be ascertained by examining any of our standard works of reference. They give accurately enough the facts about the visit to Vaucouleurs, the annunciation to Charles at Chinon, the raising of the siege of Orleans and the subsequent battles, the coronation at Rheims, the capture at Compiègne, and the trial and execution at Rouen, with their dates and the names of the people concerned; but they all break down on the melodramatic legend of the wicked bishop and the entrapped maiden and the rest of it. It would be far less misleading if they were wrong as to the facts, and right in their view of the facts. As it is, they illustrate the too little considered truth that the fashion in which we think changes like the fashion of our clothes, and that it is difficult, if not impossible, for most people to think otherwise than in the fashion of their own period.

HISTORY ALWAYS OUT OF DATE

This, by the way, is why children are never taught contemporary history. Their history books deal with periods of which the thinking has passed out of fashion, and the circumstances no longer apply to active life. For example, they are taught history about Washington, and told lies about Lenin. In Washington's time they were told lies (the same lies) about Washington, and taught history about Cromwell. In the fifteenth and sixteenth centuries they were told lies about Joan, and by this time might very well be told the truth about her. Unfortunately the lies did not cease when the political circumstances became obsolete. The Reformation, which Joan had unconsciously anticipated, kept the questions which arose in her case burning up to our own day (you can see plenty of the burnt houses still in Ireland), with the result that Joan has remained the subject of anti-Clerical lies, of specifically Protestant lies, and of Roman Catholic evasions of her unconscious Protestantism. The truth sticks in our throats with all the sauces it is served with: it will never go down until we take it without any sauce at all.

THE REAL JOAN NOT MARVELLOUS
ENOUGH FOR US

But even in its simplicity, the faith demanded by Joan is one
which the anti-metaphysical temper of nineteenth century civilization, which remains powerful in England and America, and
is tyrannical in France, contemptuously refuses her. We do not,
like her contemporaries, rush to the opposite extreme in a recoil
from her as from a witch self-sold to the devil, because we do
not believe in the devil nor in the possibility of commercial
contracts with him. Our credulity, though enormous, is not
boundless; and our stock of it is quite used up by our mediums,
clairvoyants, hand readers, slate writers, Christian Scientists,
psycho-analysts, electronic vibration diviners, therapeutists of
all schools registered and unregistered, astrologers, astronomers
who tell us that the sun is nearly a hundred million miles away
and that Betelgeuse is ten times as big as the whole universe,
physicists who balance Betelgeuse by describing the incredible
smallness of the atom, and a host of other marvel mongers
whose credulity would have dissolved the Middle Ages in a roar
of sceptical merriment. In the Middle Ages people believed that
the earth was flat, for which they had at least the evidence of
their senses: we believe it to be round, not because as many as
one per cent of us could give the physical reasons for so quaint
a belief, but because modern science has convinced us that
nothing that is obvious is true, and that everything that is
magical, improbable, extraordinary, gigantic, microscopic,
heartless, or outrageous is scientific.

I must not, by the way, be taken as implying that the earth is
flat, or that all or any of our amazing credulities are delusions
or impostures. I am only defending my own age against the
charge of being less imaginative than the Middle Ages. I affirm
that the nineteenth century, and still more the twentieth, can
knock the fifteenth into a cocked hat in point of susceptibility
to marvels and miracles and saints and prophets and magicians
and monsters and fairy tales of all kinds. The proportion of

marvel to immediately credible statement in the latest edition of the Encyclopædia Britannica is enormously greater than in the Bible. The medieval doctors of divinity who did not pretend to settle how many angels could dance on the point of a needle cut a very poor figure as far as romantic credulity is concerned beside the modern physicists who have settled to the billionth of a millimetre every movement and position in the dance of the electrons. Not for worlds would I question the precise accuracy of these calculations or the existence of electrons (whatever they may be). The fate of Joan is a warning to me against such heresy. But why the men who believe in electrons should regard themselves as less credulous than the men who believed in angels is not apparent to me. If they refuse to believe, with the Rouen assessors of 1431, that Joan was a witch, it is not because that explanation is too marvellous, but because it is not marvellous enough.

THE STAGE LIMITS OF HISTORICAL REPRESENTATION

For the story of Joan I refer the reader to the play which follows. It contains all that need be known about her; but as it is for stage use I have had to condense into three and a half hours a series of events which in their historical happening were spread over four times as many months; for the theatre imposes unities of time and place from which Nature in her boundless wastefulness is free. Therefore the reader must not suppose that Joan really put Robert de Baudricourt in her pocket in fifteen minutes, nor that her excommunication, recantation, relapse, and death at the stake were a matter of half an hour or so. Neither do I claim more for my dramatizations of Joan's contemporaries than that some of them are probably slightly more like the originals than those imaginary portraits of all the Popes from Saint Peter onward through the Dark Ages which are still gravely exhibited in the Uffizi in Florence (or were when I was there last). My Dunois would do equally well for the Duc d'Alençon.

Both left descriptions of Joan so similar that, as a man always describes himself unconsciously whenever he describes anyone else, I have inferred that these goodnatured young men were very like one another in mind; so I have lumped the twain into a single figure, thereby saving the theatre manager a salary and a suit of armor. Dunois' face, still on record at Châteaudun, is a suggestive help. But I really know no more about these men and their circle than Shakespear knew about Falconbridge and the Duke of Austria, or about Macbeth and Macduff. In view of things they did in history, and have to do again in the play, I can only invent appropriate characters for them in Shakespear's manner.

A VOID IN THE ELIZABETHAN DRAMA

I have, however, one advantage over the Elizabethans. I write in full view of the Middle Ages, which may be said to have been rediscovered in the middle of the nineteenth century after an eclipse of about four hundred and fifty years. The Renascence of antique literature and art in the sixteenth century, and the lusty growth of Capitalism, between them buried the Middle Ages; and their resurrection is a second Renascence. Now there is not a breath of medieval atmosphere in Shakespear's histories. His John of Gaunt is like a study of the old age of Drake. Although he was a Catholic by family tradition, his figures are all intensely Protestant, individualist, sceptical, self-centred in everything but their love affairs, and completely personal and selfish even in them. His kings are not statesmen: his cardinals have no religion: a novice can read his plays from one end to the other without learning that the world is finally governed by forces expressing themselves in religions and laws which make epochs rather than by vulgarly ambitious individuals who make rows. The divinity which shapes our ends, rough hew them how we will, is mentioned fatalistically only to be forgotten immediately like a passing vague apprehension. To Shakespear as to Mark Twain, Cauchon would have been a tyrant and a bully instead of a Catholic, and the inquisitor Lemaître would

have been a Sadist instead of a lawyer. Warwick would have
had no more feudal quality than his successor the King Maker
has in the play of Henry VI. We should have seen them all
completely satisfied that if they would only to their own selves
be true they could not then be false to any man (a precept which
represents the reaction against medievalism at its intensest) as if
they were beings in the air, without public responsibilities of
any kind. All Shakespear's characters are so: that is why they
seem natural to our middle classes, who are comfortable and
irresponsible at other people's expense, and are neither ashamed
of that condition nor even conscious of it. Nature abhors this
vacuum in Shakespear; and I have taken care to let the medieval
atmosphere blow through my play freely. Those who see it
performed will not mistake the startling event it records for a
mere personal accident. They will have before them not only
the visible and human puppets, but the Church, the Inquisition,
the Feudal System, with divine inspiration always beating
against their too inelastic limits: all more terrible in their dramatic force than any of the little mortal figures clanking about
in plate armor or moving silently in the frocks and hoods of the
order of St Dominic.

TRAGEDY, NOT MELODRAMA

There are no villains in the piece. Crime, like disease, is not
interesting: it is something to be done away with by general
consent, and that is all about it. It is what men do at their best,
with good intentions, and what normal men and women find
that they must and will do in spite of their intentions, that really
concern us. The rascally bishop and the cruel inquisitor of Mark
Twain and Andrew Lang are as dull as pickpockets; and they
reduce Joan to the level of the even less interesting person whose
pocket is picked. I have represented both of them as capable
and eloquent exponents of The Church Militant and The Church
Litigant, because only by doing so can I maintain my drama on
the level of high tragedy and save it from becoming a mere police
court sensation. A villain in a play can never be anything more

than a *diabolus ex machina*, possibly a more exciting expedient than a *deus ex machina*, but both equally mechanical, and therefore interesting only as mechanism. It is, I repeat, what normally innocent people do that concerns us; and if Joan had not been burnt by normally innocent people in the energy of their righteousness her death at their hands would have no more significance than the Tokyo earthquake, which burnt a great many maidens. The tragedy of such murders is that they are not committed by murderers. They are judicial murders, pious murders; and this contradiction at once brings an element of comedy into the tragedy: the angels may weep at the murder, but the gods laugh at the murderers.

THE INEVITABLE FLATTERIES
OF TRAGEDY

Here then we have a reason why my drama of Saint Joan's career, though it may give the essential truth of it, gives an inexact picture of some accidental facts. It goes almost without saying that the old Jeanne d'Arc melodramas, reducing everything to a conflict of villain and hero, or in Joan's case villain and heroine, not only miss the point entirely, but falsify the characters, making Cauchon a scoundrel, Joan a prima donna, and Dunois a lover. But the writer of high tragedy and comedy, aiming at the innermost attainable truth, must needs flatter Cauchon nearly as much as the melodramatist vilifies him. Although there is, as far as I have been able to discover, nothing against Cauchon that convicts him of bad faith or exceptional severity in his judicial relations with Joan, or of as much anti-prisoner, pro-police, class and sectarian bias as we now take for granted in our own courts, yet there is hardly more warrant for classing him as a great Catholic churchman, completely proof against the passions roused by the temporal situation. Neither does the inquisitor Lemaître, in such scanty accounts of him as are now recoverable, appear quite so able a master of his duties and of the case before him as I have given him credit for being.

But it is the business of the stage to make its figures more intelligible to themselves than they would be in real life; for by no other means can they be made intelligible to the audience. And in this case Cauchon and Lemaître have to make intelligible not only themselves but the Church and the Inquisition, just as Warwick has to make the feudal system intelligible, the three between them having thus to make a twentieth century audience conscious of an epoch fundamentally different from its own. Obviously the real Cauchon, Lemaître, and Warwick could not have done this: they were part of the Middle Ages themselves, and therefore as unconscious of its peculiarities as of the atomic formula of the air they breathed. But the play would be unintelligible if I had not endowed them with enough of this consciousness to enable them to explain their attitude to the twentieth century. All I claim is that by this inevitable sacrifice of verisimilitude I have secured in the only possible way sufficient veracity to justify me in claiming that as far as I can gather from the available documentation, and from such powers of divination as I possess, the things I represent these three exponents of the drama as saying are the things they actually would have said if they had known what they were really doing. And beyond this neither drama nor history can go in my hands.

SOME WELL-MEANT PROPOSALS FOR THE IMPROVEMENT OF THE PLAY

I have to thank several critics on both sides of the Atlantic, including some whose admiration for my play is most generously enthusiastic, for their heartfelt instructions as to how it can be improved. They point out that by the excision of the epilogue and all the references to such undramatic and tedious matters as the Church, the feudal system, the Inquisition, the theory of heresy and so forth, all of which, they point out, would be ruthlessly blue pencilled by any experienced manager, the play could be considerably shortened. I think they are mistaken. The experienced knights of the blue pencil, having saved an hour and a half by disembowelling the play, would at once proceed to waste two hours in building elaborate scenery, having real water in the river Loire and a real bridge across it, and staging an obviously sham fight for possession of it, with the victorious French led by Joan on a real horse. The coronation would eclipse all previous theatrical displays, shewing, first, the procession through the streets of Rheims, and then the service in the cathedral, with special music written for both. Joan would be burnt on the stage, as Mr Matheson Lang always is in The Wandering Jew, on the principle that it does not matter in the least why a woman is burnt provided she is burnt, and people can pay to see it done. The intervals between the acts whilst these splendors were being built up and then demolished by the stage carpenters would seem eternal, to the great profit of the refreshment bars. And the weary and demoralized audience would lose their last trains and curse me for writing such inordinately long and intolerably dreary and meaningless plays. But the applause of the press would be unanimous. Nobody who knows the stage history of Shakespear will doubt that this is what would happen if I knew my business so little as to listen to these well intentioned but disastrous counsellors: indeed it probably will happen when I am no longer in control of the performing rights. So perhaps it will be as well for the public to see the play while I am still alive.

THE EPILOGUE

As to the epilogue, I could hardly be expected to stultify myself by implying that Joan's history in the world ended unhappily with her execution, instead of beginning there. It was necessary by hook or crook to shew the canonized Joan as well as the incinerated one; for many a woman has got herself burnt by carelessly whisking a muslin skirt into the drawing room fireplace, but getting canonized is a different matter, and a more important one. So I am afraid the epilogue must stand.

TO THE CRITICS, LEST THEY SHOULD
FEEL IGNORED

To a professional critic (I have been one myself) theatre-going is the curse of Adam. The play is the evil he is paid to endure in the sweat of his brow; and the sooner it is over, the better. This would seem to place him in irreconcilable opposition to the paying playgoer, from whose point of view the longer the play, the more entertainment he gets for his money. It does in fact so place him, especially in the provinces, where the playgoer goes to the theatre for the sake of the play solely, and insists so effectively on a certain number of hours' entertainment that touring managers are sometimes seriously embarrassed by the brevity of the London plays they have to deal in.

For in London the critics are reinforced by a considerable body of persons who go to the theatre as many others go to church, to display their best clothes and compare them with other people's; to be in the fashion, and have something to talk about at dinner parties; to adore a pet performer; to pass the evening anywhere rather than at home: in short, for any or every reason except interest in dramatic art as such. In fashionable centres the number of irreligious people who go to church, of unmusical people who go to concerts and operas, and of undramatic people who go to the theatre, is so prodigious that sermons have been cut down to ten minutes and plays to two hours; and, even at that, congregations sit longing for the benediction and audiences for the final curtain, so that they may get away to the lunch or supper they really crave for, after arriving as late as (or later than) the hour of beginning can possibly be made for them.

Thus from the stalls and in the Press an atmosphere of hypocrisy spreads. Nobody says straight out that genuine drama is a tedious nuisance, and that to ask people to endure more than two hours of it (with two long intervals of relief) is an intolerable imposition. Nobody says 'I hate classical tragedy and comedy as I hate sermons and symphonies; but I like police news and divorce news and any kind of dancing or decoration that has an aphrodisiac effect on me or on my wife or husband. And whatever superior people may pretend, I cannot associate pleasure with any sort of intellectual activity; and I dont believe anyone else can either.' Such things are not said; yet nine-tenths of what is offered as criticism of the drama in the metropolitan Press of Europe and America is nothing but a muddled paraphrase of it. If it does not mean that, it means nothing.

I do not complain of this, though it complains very unreasonably of me. But I can take no more notice of it than Einstein of the people who are incapable of mathematics. I write in the classical manner for those who pay for admission to a theatre because they like classical comedy or tragedy for its own sake, and like it so much when it is good of its kind and well done that they tear themselves away from it with reluctance to catch the very latest train or omnibus that will take them home. Far from arriving late from an eight or half-past eight o'clock dinner so as to escape at least the first half-hour of the performance, they stand in queues outside the theatre doors for hours beforehand in bitingly cold weather to secure a seat. In countries where a play lasts a week, they bring baskets of provisions and sit it out. These are the patrons on whom I depend for my bread. I do not give them performances twelve hours long, because circumstances do not at present make such entertainments feasible; though a performance beginning after breakfast and ending at sunset is as possible physically and artistically in Surrey or Middlesex as in Ober-Ammergau; and an all-night sitting in a theatre would be at least as enjoyable as an all-night sitting in the House of Commons, and much more useful. But in St Joan I have done my best by going to the well-established classical limit of three and a half hours' practically continuous playing, barring the one interval imposed by considerations which have nothing to do with art. I know that this is hard on the pseudo-critics and on the fashionable people whose playgoing is a hypocrisy. I cannot help feeling some compassion for them when they assure me that my play, though a great play, must fail hopelessly, because it does not begin at a quarter to nine and end at eleven. The facts are overwhelmingly against them. They forget that all men are not as they are. Still, I am sorry for them; and though I cannot for their sakes undo my work and help the people who hate the theatre to drive out the people who love it, yet I may point out to them that they have several remedies in their own hands. They can escape the first part of the play by their usual practice of arriving late. They can escape the epilogue by not waiting for it. And if the irreducible minimum thus attained is still too painful, they can stay away altogether. But I deprecate this extreme course, because it is good neither for my pocket nor for their own souls. Already a few of them, noticing that what matters is not the absolute length of time occupied by a play, but the speed with which that time passes, are discovering that the theatre, though purgatorial in its Aristotelian moments, is not necessarily always the dull place they have so often found it. What do its discomforts matter when the play makes us forget them?

AYOT ST LAWRENCE   *May 1924*

SAINT JOAN

SCENE I

A fine spring morning on the river Meuse, between Lorraine and Champagne, in the year 1429 AD, in the castle of Vaucouleurs.

Captain Robert de Baudricourt, a military squire, handsome and physically energetic, but with no will of his own, is disguising that defect in his usual fashion by storming terribly at his steward, a trodden worm, scanty of flesh, scanty of hair, who might be any age from 18 to 55, being the sort of man whom age cannot wither because he has never bloomed.

The two are in a sunny stone chamber on the first floor of the castle. At a plain strong oak table, seated in chair to match, the captain presents his left profile. The steward stands facing him at the other side of the table, if so deprecatory a stance as his can be called standing. The mullioned thirteenth century window is open behind him. Near it in the corner is a turret with a narrow arched doorway leading to a winding stair which descends to the courtyard. There is a stout fourlegged stool under the table, and a wooden chest under the window.

ROBERT. No eggs! No eggs!! Thousand thunders, man, what do you mean by no eggs?

STEWARD. Sir: it is not my fault. It is the act of God.

ROBERT. Blasphemy. You tell me there are no eggs; and you blame your Maker for it.

STEWARD. Sir: what can I do? I cannot lay eggs.

ROBERT [*sarcastic*] Ha! You jest about it.

STEWARD. No, sir, God knows. We all have to go without eggs just as you have, sir. The hens will not lay.

ROBERT. Indeed! [*Rising*] Now listen to me, you.

STEWARD [*humbly*] Yes, sir.

ROBERT. What am I?

STEWARD. What are you, sir?

ROBERT [*coming at him*] Yes: what am I? Am I Robert, squire of Baudricourt and captain of this castle of Vaucouleurs; or am I a cowboy?

[handwritten annotation: not an anachronism (ie Annie Oakley etc)]

STEWARD. Oh, sir, you know you are a greater man here than the king himself.

ROBERT. Precisely. And now, do you know what you are?

STEWARD. I am nobody, sir, except that I have the honor to be your steward.

ROBERT [*driving him to the wall, adjective by adjective*] You have not only the honor of being my steward, but the privilege of being the worst, most incompetent, drivelling snivelling jibbering jabbering idiot of a steward in France. [*He strides back to the table*].

STEWARD [*cowering on the chest*] Yes, sir: to a great man like you I must seem like that.

ROBERT [*turning*] My fault, I suppose. Eh?

STEWARD [*coming to him deprecatingly*] Oh, sir: you always give my most innocent words such a turn!

ROBERT. I will give your neck a turn if you dare tell me, when I ask you how many eggs there are, that you cannot lay any.

STEWARD [*protesting*] Oh sir, oh sir –

ROBERT. No: not oh sir, oh sir, but no sir, no sir. My three Barbary hens and the black are the best layers in Champagne. And you come and tell me that there are no eggs! Who stole them? Tell me that, before I kick you out through the castle gate for a liar and a seller of my goods to thieves. The milk was short yesterday, too: do not forget that.

STEWARD [*desperate*] I know, sir. I know only too well. There is no milk: there are no eggs: tomorrow there will be nothing.

ROBERT. Nothing! You will steal the lot: eh?

STEWARD. No, sir: nobody will steal anything. But there is a spell on us: we are bewitched.

ROBERT. That story is not good enough for me. Robert de Baudricourt burns witches and hangs thieves. Go. Bring me four dozen eggs and two gallons of milk here in this room before noon, or Heaven have mercy on your bones! I will teach you to make a fool of me. [*He resumes his seat with an air of finality*].

STEWARD. Sir: I tell you there are no eggs. There will be none – not if you were to kill me for it – as long as The Maid is at the door.

ROBERT. The Maid! What maid? What are you talking about?

STEWARD. The girl from Lorraine, sir. From Domrémy.

ROBERT [*rising in fearful wrath*] Thirty thousand thunders! Fifty thousand devils! Do you mean to say that that girl, who had the impudence to ask to see me two days ago, and whom I told you to send back to her father with my orders that he was to give her a good hiding, is here still?

STEWARD. I have told her to go, sir. She wont.

ROBERT. I did not tell you to tell her to go: I told you to throw her out. You have fifty men-at-arms and a dozen lumps of able-bodied servants to carry out my orders. Are they afraid of her?

STEWARD. She is so positive, sir.

ROBERT [*seizing him by the scruff of the neck*] Positive! Now see here. I am going to throw you downstairs.

STEWARD. No, sir. Please.

ROBERT. Well, stop me by being positive. It's quite easy: any slut of a girl can do it.

STEWARD [*hanging limp in his hands*] Sir, sir: you cannot get rid of h e r by throwing m e out. [*Robert has to let him drop. He squats on his knees on the floor, contemplating his master resignedly*]. You see, sir, you are much more positive than I am. But so is she.

ROBERT. I am stronger than you are, you fool.

STEWARD. No, sir: it isnt that: it's your strong character, sir. She is weaker than we are: she is only a slip of a girl; but we cannot make her go.

ROBERT. You parcel of curs: you are afraid of her.

STEWARD [*rising cautiously*] No sir: we are afraid of you; but she puts courage into us. She really doesnt seem to be afraid of anything. Perhaps you could frighten her, sir.

ROBERT [*grimly*] Perhaps. Where is she now?

STEWARD. Down in the courtyard, sir, talking to the soldiers as usual. She is always talking to the soldiers except when she is praying.

ROBERT. Praying! Ha! You believe she prays, you idiot. I know the sort of girl that is always talking to soldiers. She shall talk to me a bit. [*He goes to the window and shouts fiercely through it*] Hallo, you there!

A GIRL'S VOICE [*bright, strong, and rough*] Is it me, sir?

ROBERT. Yes, you.

THE VOICE. Be you captain?

ROBERT. Yes, damn your impudence, I be captain. Come up here. [*To the soldiers in the yard*] Shew her the way, you. And shove her along quick. [*He leaves the window, and returns to his place at the table, where he sits magisterially*].

STEWARD [*whispering*] She wants to go and be a soldier herself. She wants you to give her soldier's clothes. Armor, sir! And a sword! Actually! [*He steals behind Robert*].

Joan appears in the turret doorway. She is an ablebodied country girl of 17 or 18, respectably dressed in red, with an uncommon face; eyes very wide apart and bulging as they often do in very imaginative people, a long well-shaped nose with wide nostrils, a short upper lip, resolute but full-lipped mouth, and handsome fighting chin. She comes eagerly to the table, delighted at having penetrated to Baudricourt's presence at last, and full of hope as to the result. His scowl does not check or frighten her in the least. Her voice is normally a hearty coaxing voice, very confident, very appealing, very hard to resist.

JOAN [*bobbing a curtsey*] Good morning, captain squire. Captain: you are to give me a horse and armor and some soldiers, and send me to the Dauphin. Those are your orders from my Lord.

ROBERT [*outraged*] Orders from y o u r lord! And who the devil may your lord be? Go back to him, and tell him that I am neither duke nor peer at his orders: I am squire of Baudricourt; and I take no orders except from the king.

JOAN [*reassuringly*] Yes, squire: that is all right. My Lord is the King of Heaven.

ROBERT. Why, the girl's mad. [*To the steward*] Why didn't you tell me so, you blockhead?

STEWARD. Sir: do not anger her: give her what she wants.

JOAN [*impatient, but friendly*] They all say I am mad until I talk to them, squire. But you see that it is the will of God that you are to do what He has put into my mind.

ROBERT. It is the will of God that I shall send you back to your father with orders to put you under lock and key and thrash the madness out of you. What have you to say to that?

JOAN. You think you will, squire; but you will find it all coming quite different. You said you would not see me; but here I am.

STEWARD [*appealing*] Yes, sir. You see, sir.

ROBERT. Hold your tongue, you.

STEWARD [*abjectly*] Yes, sir.

ROBERT [*to Joan, with a sour loss of confidence*] So you are presuming on my seeing you, are you?

JOAN [*sweetly*] Yes, squire.

ROBERT [*feeling that he has lost ground, brings down his two fists squarely on the table, and inflates his chest imposingly to cure the unwelcome and only too familiar sensation*] Now listen to me. I am going to assert myself.

JOAN [*busily*] Please do, squire. The horse will cost sixteen francs. It is a good deal of money: but I can save it on the armor. I can find a soldier's armor that will fit me well enough: I am very hardy; and I do not need beautiful armor made to my measure like you wear. I shall not want many soldiers: the Dauphin will give me all I need to raise the siege of Orleans.

ROBERT [*flabbergasted*] To raise the siege of Orleans!

JOAN [*simply*] Yes, squire: that is what God is sending me to do. Three men will be enough for you to send with me if they are good men and gentle to me. They have promised to come with me. Polly and Jack and –

ROBERT. Polly!! You impudent baggage, do you dare call squire Bertrand de Poulengey Polly to my face?

JOAN. His friends call him so, squire: I did not know he had any other name. Jack –

ROBERT. That is Monsieur John of Metz, I suppose?

JOAN. Yes, squire. Jack will come willingly: he is a very kind gentleman, and gives me money to give to the poor. I think John Godsave will come, and Dick the Archer, and their servants John of Honecourt and Julian. There will be no trouble for you, squire: I have arranged it all: you have only to give the order.

ROBERT [*contemplating her in a stupor of amazement*] Well, I a m damned!

JOAN [*with unruffled sweetness*] No, squire: God is very merciful; and the blessed saints Catherine and Margaret, who speak to me every day [*he gapes*], will intercede for you. You will go to paradise; and your name will be remembered for ever as my first helper.

ROBERT [*to the steward, still much bothered, but changing his tone as he pursues a new clue*] Is this true about Monsieur de Poulengey?

STEWARD [*eagerly*] Yes, sir, and about Monsieur de Metz too. They both want to go with her.

ROBERT [*thoughtful*] Mf! [*He goes to the window, and shouts into the courtyard*] Hallo! You there: send Monsieur de Poulengey to me, will you? [*He turns to Joan*] Get out; and wait in the yard.

JOAN [*smiling brightly at him*] Right, squire. [*She goes out*].

ROBERT [*to the steward*] Go with her, you, you dithering imbecile. Stay within call; and keep your eye on her. I shall have her up here again.

STEWARD. Do so in God's name, sir. Think of those hens, the best layers in Champagne; and –

ROBERT. Think of my boot; and take your backside out of reach of it.

The steward retreats hastily and finds himself confronted in the doorway by Bertrand de Poulengey, a lymphatic French gentleman-at-arms, aged 36 or thereabout, employed in the department of the provost-marshal, dreamily absent-minded, seldom speaking unless spoken to, and then slow and obstinate in reply; altogether in contrast to the self-assertive, loud-mouthed, superficially energetic, fundamentally will-less Robert. The steward makes way for him, and vanishes.

Poulengey salutes, and stands awaiting orders.

ROBERT [*genially*] It isnt service, Polly. A friendly talk. Sit down. [*He hooks the stool from under the table with his instep*].

Poulengey, relaxing, comes into the room; places the stool between the table and the window; and sits down ruminatively. Robert, half sitting on the end of the table, begins the friendly talk.

ROBERT. Now listen to me, Polly. I must talk to you like a
father.

    *Poulengey looks up at him gravely for a moment, but says
nothing.*

ROBERT. It's about this girl you are interested in. Now, I have
seen her. I have talked to her. First, she's mad. That doesnt
matter. Second, she's not a farm wench. She's a bourgeoise.
That matters a good deal. I know her class exactly. Her father
came here last year to represent his village in a lawsuit: he is
one of their notables. A farmer. Not a gentleman farmer: he
makes money by it, and lives by it. Still, not a laborer. Not a
mechanic. He might have a cousin a lawyer, or in the Church.
People of this sort may be of no account socially; but they can
give a lot of bother to the authorities. That is to say, to m e.
Now no doubt it seems to you a very simple thing to take this
girl away, humbugging her into the belief that you are taking
her to the Dauphin. But if you get her into trouble, you may
get m e into no end of a mess, as I am her father's lord, and
responsible for her protection. So friends or no friends, Polly,
hands off her.

POULENGEY [*with deliberate impressiveness*] I should as soon
think of the Blessed Virgin herself in that way, as of this girl.

ROBERT [*coming off the table*] But she says you and Jack and
Dick have offered to go with her. What for? You are not
going to tell me that you take her crazy notion of going to the
Dauphin seriously, are you?

POULENGEY [*slowly*] There is something about her. They are
pretty foulmouthed and foulminded down there in the guard-
room, some of them. But there hasnt been a word that has
anything to do with her being a woman. They have stopped
swearing before her. There is something. Something. It may
be worth trying.

ROBERT. Oh, come, Polly! pull yourself together. Commonsense was never your strong point; but this is a little too much.
[*He retreats disgustedly*].

POULENGEY [*unmoved*] What is the good of commonsense? If
we had any commonsense we should join the Duke of Burgundy and the English king. They hold half the country, right

down to the Loire. They have Paris. They have this castle: you know very well that we had to surrender it to the Duke of Bedford, and that you are only holding it on parole. The Dauphin is in Chinon, like a rat in a corner, except that he wont fight. We dont even know that he is the Dauphin: his mother says he isnt; and she ought to know. Think of that! the queen denying the legitimacy of her own son!

ROBERT. Well, she married her daughter to the English king. Can you blame the woman?

POULENGEY. I blame nobody. But thanks to her, the Dauphin is down and out; and we may as well face it. The English will take Orleans: the Bastard will not be able to stop them.

ROBERT. He beat the English the year before last at Montargis. I was with him.

POULENGEY. No matter: his men are cowed now; and he cant work miracles. And I tell you that nothing can save our side now but a miracle.

ROBERT. Miracles are all right, Polly. The only difficulty about them is that they dont happen nowadays.

POULENGEY. I used to think so. I am not so sure now. [*Rising, and moving ruminatively towards the window*] At all events this is not a time to leave any stone unturned. There is something about the girl.

ROBERT. Oh! You think the girl can work miracles, do you?

POULENGEY. I think the girl herself is a bit of a miracle. Anyhow, she is the last card left in our hand. Better play her than throw up the game. [*He wanders to the turret*].

ROBERT [*wavering*] You really think that?

POULENGEY [*turning*] Is there anything else left for us to think?

ROBERT [*going to him*] Look here, Polly. If you were in my place would you let a girl like that do you out of sixteen francs for a horse?

POULENGEY. I will pay for the horse.

ROBERT. You will!

POULENGEY. Yes: I will back my opinion.

ROBERT. You will really gamble on a forlorn hope to the tune of sixteen francs?

POULENGEY. It is not a gamble.

ROBERT. What else is it?

POULENGEY. It is a certainty. Her words and her ardent faith in God have put fire into me.

ROBERT [*giving him up*] Whew! You are as mad as she is.

POULENGEY [*obstinately*] We want a few mad people now. See where the sane ones have landed us!

ROBERT [*his irresoluteness now openly swamping his affected decisiveness*] I shall feel like a precious fool. Still, if you feel sure – ?

POULENGEY. I feel sure enough to take her to Chinon – unless you stop me.

ROBERT. This is not fair. You are putting the responsibility on me. *Lack of will.*

POULENGEY. It is on you whichever way you decide.

ROBERT. Yes: thats just it. Which way am I to decide? You dont see how awkward this is for me. [*Snatching at a dilatory step with an unconscious hope that Joan will make up his mind for him*] Do you think I ought to have another talk to her?

POULENGEY [*rising*] Yes. [*He goes to the window and calls*] Joan!

JOAN'S VOICE. Will he let us go, Polly?

POULENGEY. Come up. Come in. [*Turning to Robert*] Shall I leave you with her?

ROBERT. No: stay here; and back me up.

Poulengey sits down on the chest. Robert goes back to his magisterial chair, but remains standing to inflate himself more imposingly. Joan comes in, full of good news.

JOAN. Jack will go halves for the horse.

ROBERT. Well!! [*He sits, deflated*].

POULENGEY [*gravely*] Sit down, Joan.

JOAN [*checked a little, and looking to Robert*] May I?

ROBERT. Do what you are told.

Joan curtsies and sits down on the stool between them. Robert outfaces his perplexity with his most peremptory air.

ROBERT. What is your name?

JOAN [*chattily*] They always call me Jenny in Lorraine. Here in France I am Joan. The soldiers call me The Maid.

ROBERT. What is your surname?

JOAN. Surname? What is that? My father sometimes calls himself d'Arc; but I know nothing about it. You met my father.
He –

ROBERT. Yes, yes; I remember. You come from Domrémy in
Lorraine, I think.

JOAN. Yes; but what does it matter? we all speak French.

ROBERT. Dont ask questions: answer them. How old are you?

JOAN. Seventeen: so they tell me. It might be nineteen. I dont
remember.

ROBERT. What did you mean when you said that St Catherine
and St Margaret talked to you every day?

JOAN. They do.

ROBERT. What are they like?

JOAN [*suddenly obstinate*] I will tell you nothing about that:
they have not given me leave.

ROBERT. But you actually see them; and they talk to you just
as I am talking to you?

JOAN. No: it is quite different. I cannot tell you: you must not
talk to me about my voices.

ROBERT. How do you mean? voices?

JOAN. I hear voices telling me what to do. They come from
God.

ROBERT. They come from your imagination.

JOAN. Of course. That is how the messages of God come to us.

POULENGEY. Checkmate.

ROBERT. No fear! [*To Joan*] So God says you are to raise the
siege of Orleans?

JOAN. And to crown the Dauphin in Rheims Cathedral.

ROBERT [*gasping*] Crown the D—! Gosh!

JOAN. And to make the English leave France.

ROBERT [*sarcastic*] Anything else?

JOAN [*charming*] Not just at present, thank you, squire.

ROBERT. I suppose you think raising a siege is as easy as chasing
a cow out of a meadow. You think soldiering is anybody's
job?

JOAN. I do not think it can be very difficult if God is on your
side, and you are willing to put your life in His hand. But
many soldiers are very simple.

ROBERT [*grimly*] Simple! Did you ever see English soldiers fighting?

JOAN. They are only men. God made them just like us; but He gave them their own country and their own language; and it is not His will that they should come into our country and try to speak our language.

ROBERT. Who has been putting such nonsense into your head? Dont you know that soldiers are subject to their feudal lord, and that it is nothing to them or to you whether he is the duke of Burgundy or the king of England or the king of France? What has their language to do with it?

JOAN. I do not understand that a bit. We are all subject to the King of Heaven; and He gave us our countries and our languages, and meant us to keep to them. If it were not so it would be murder to kill an Englishman in battle; and you, squire, would be in great danger of hell fire. You must not think about your duty to your feudal lord, but about your duty to God.

POULENGEY. It's no use, Robert: she can choke you like that every time.

ROBERT. Can she, by Saint Denis! We shall see. [*To Joan*] We are not talking about God: we are talking about practical affairs. I ask you again, girl, have you ever seen English soldiers fighting? Have you ever seen them plundering, burning, turning the countryside into a desert? Have you heard no tales of their Black Prince who was blacker than the devil himself, or of the English king's father?

JOAN. You must not be afraid, Robert –

ROBERT. Damn you, I am not afraid. And who gave you leave to call me Robert?

JOAN. You were called so in church in the name of our Lord. All the other names are your father's or your brother's or anybody's.

ROBERT. Tcha!

JOAN. Listen to me, squire. At Domrémy we had to fly to the next village to escape from the English soldiers. Three of them were left behind, wounded. I came to know these three poor goddams quite well. They had not half my strength.

ROBERT. Do you know why they are called goddams?

JOAN. No. Everyone calls them goddams.

ROBERT. It is because they are always calling on their God to condemn their souls to perdition. That is what goddam means in their language. How do you like it?

JOAN. God will be merciful to them; and they will act like His good children when they go back to the country He made for them, and made them for. I have heard the tales of the Black Prince. The moment he touched the soil of our country the devil entered into him, and made him a black fiend. But at home, in the place made for him by God, he was good. It is always so. If I went into England against the will of God to conquer England, and tried to live there and speak its language, the devil would enter into me; and when I was old I should shudder to remember the wickednesses I did.

ROBERT. Perhaps. But the more devil you were the better you might fight. That is why the goddams will take Orleans. And you cannot stop them, nor ten thousand like you.

JOAN. One thousand like me can stop them. Ten like me can stop them with God on our side. [She rises impetuously, and goes at him, unable to sit quiet any longer]. You do not understand, squire. Our soldiers are always beaten because they are fighting only to save their skins; and the shortest way to save your skin is to run away. Our knights are thinking only of the money they will make in ransoms: it is not kill or be killed with them, but pay or be paid. But I will teach them all to fight that the will of God may be done in France; and then they will drive the poor goddams before them like sheep. You and Polly will live to see the day when there will not be an English soldier on the soil of France; and there will be but one king there: not the feudal English king, but God's French one.

ROBERT [to Poulengey] This may be all rot, Polly; but the troops might swallow it, though nothing that we can say seems able to put any fight into them. Even the Dauphin might swallow it. And if she can put fight into him, she can put it into anybody.

POULENGEY. I can see no harm in trying. Can you? And there is something about the girl –

ROBERT [*turning to Joan*] Now listen you to me; and [*desperately*] dont cut in before I have time to think.

JOAN [*plumping down on the stool again, like an obedient schoolgirl*] Yes, squire.

ROBERT. Your orders are, that you are to go to Chinon under the escort of this gentleman and three of his friends.

JOAN [*radiant, clasping her hands*] Oh, squire! Your head is all circled with light, like a saint's.

POULENGEY. How is she to get into the royal presence?

ROBERT [*who has looked up for his halo rather apprehensively*] I dont know: how did she get into my presence? If the Dauphin can keep her out he is a better man than I take him for. [*Rising*] I will send her to Chinon; and she can say I sent her. Then let come what may: I can do no more.

JOAN. And the dress? I may have a soldier's dress, maynt I, squire?

ROBERT. Have what you please. I wash my hands of it. *Pilate*

JOAN [*wildly excited by her success*] Come, Polly. [*She dashes out*].

ROBERT [*shaking Poulengey's hand*] Goodbye, old man, I am taking a big chance. Few other men would have done it. But as you say, there is something about her.

POULENGEY. Yes: there is something about her. Goodbye. [*He goes out*].

    Robert, still very doubtful whether he has not been made a fool of by a crazy female, and a social inferior to boot, scratches his head and slowly comes back from the door.

    The steward runs in with a basket.

STEWARD. Sir, sir –

ROBERT. What now?

STEWARD. The hens are laying like mad, sir. Five dozen eggs!

ROBERT [*stiffens convulsively: crosses himself: and forms with his pale lips the words*] Christ in heaven! [*Aloud but breathless*] She d i d come from God.

Egg shortage until she was granted what she was denied.

SCENE II

Chinon, in Touraine. An end of the throne room in the castle, curtained off to make an antechamber. The Archbishop of Rheims, close on 50, a full-fed prelate with nothing of the ecclesiastic about him except his imposing bearing, and the Lord Chamberlain, Monseigneur de la Trémouille, a monstrous arrogant wineskin of a man, are waiting for the Dauphin. There is a door in the wall to the right of the two men. It is late in the afternoon on the 8th of March, 1429. The Archbishop stands with dignity whilst the Chamberlain, on his left, fumes about in the worst of tempers.

LA TRÉMOUILLE. What the devil does the Dauphin mean by keeping us waiting like this? I dont know how you have the patience to stand there like a stone idol.

THE ARCHBISHOP. You see, I am an archbishop; and an archbishop is a sort of idol. At any rate he has to learn to keep still and suffer fools patiently. Besides, my dear Lord Chamberlain, it is the Dauphin's royal privilege to keep you waiting, is it not?

LA TRÉMOUILLE. Dauphin be damned! saving your reverence. Do you know how much money he owes me?

THE ARCHBISHOP. Much more than he owes me, I have no doubt, because you are a much richer man. But I take it he owes you all you could afford to lend him. That is what he owes me.

LA TRÉMOUILLE. Twenty-seven thousand: that was his last haul. A cool twenty-seven thousand!

THE ARCHBISHOP. What becomes of it all? He never has a suit of clothes that I would throw to a curate.

LA TRÉMOUILLE. He dines on a chicken or a scrap of mutton. He borrows my last penny; and there is nothing to shew for it. [*A page appears in the doorway*]. At last!

THE PAGE. No, my lord: it is not His Majesty. Monsieur de Rais is approaching.

LA TRÉMOUILLE. Young Bluebeard! Why announce him?

THE PAGE. Captain La Hire is with him. Something has happened, I think.

Gilles de Rais, a young man of 25, very smart and self-possessed, and sporting the extravagance of a little curled beard dyed blue at a clean-shaven court, comes in. He is determined to make himself agreeable, but lacks natural joyousness, and is not really pleasant. In fact when he defies the Church some eleven years later he is accused of trying to extract pleasure from horrible cruelties, and hanged. So far, however, there is no shadow of the gallows on him. He advances gaily to the Archbishop. The page withdraws.

BLUEBEARD. Your faithful lamb, Archbishop. Good day, my lord. Do you know what has happened to La Hire?

LA TRÉMOUILLE. He has sworn himself into a fit, perhaps.

BLUEBEARD. No: just the opposite. Foul Mouthed Frank, the only man in Touraine who could beat him at swearing, was told by a soldier that he shouldnt use such language when he was at the point of death.

THE ARCHBISHOP. Nor at any other point. But was Foul Mouthed Frank on the point of death?

BLUEBEARD. Yes: he has just fallen into a well and been drowned. La Hire is frightened out of his wits.

Captain La Hire comes in: a war dog with no court manners and pronounced camp ones.

BLUEBEARD. I have just been telling the Chamberlain and the Archbishop. The Archbishop says you are a lost man.

LA HIRE [*striding past Bluebeard, and planting himself between the Archbishop and La Trémouille*] This is nothing to joke about. It is worse than we thought. It was not a soldier, but an angel dressed as a soldier.

THE ARCHBISHOP
THE CHAMBERLAIN } [*exclaiming all together*] An angel!
BLUEBEARD

LA HIRE. Yes, an angel. She has made her way from Champagne with half a dozen men through the thick of everything: Burgundians, Goddams, deserters, robbers, and Lord knows who; and they never met a soul except the country folk. I know one of them: de Poulengey. He says she's an angel. If ever I utter an oath again may my soul be blasted to eternal damnation!

THE ARCHBISHOP. A very pious beginning, Captain.

> *Bluebeard and La Trémouille laugh at him. The page returns.*

THE PAGE. His Majesty.

> *They stand perfunctorily at court attention. The Dauphin, aged 26, really King Charles the Seventh since the death of his father, but as yet uncrowned, comes in through the curtains with a paper in his hands. He is a poor creature physically; and the current fashion of shaving closely, and hiding every scrap of hair under the headcovering or headdress, both by women and men, makes the worst of his appearance. He has little narrow eyes, near together, a long pendulous nose that droops over his thick short upper lip, and the expression of a young dog accustomed to be kicked, yet incorrigible and irrepressible. But he is neither vulgar nor stupid; and he has a cheeky humor which enables him to hold his own in conversation. Just at present he is excited, like a child with a new toy. He comes to the Archbishop's left hand. Bluebeard and La Hire retire towards the curtains.*

CHARLES. Oh, Archbishop, do you know what Robert de Baudricourt is sending me from Vaucouleurs?

THE ARCHBISHOP [*contemptuously*] I am not interested in the newest toys.

CHARLES [*indignantly*] It isnt a toy. [*Sulkily*] However, I can get on very well without your interest.

THE ARCHBISHOP. Your Highness is taking offence very unnecessarily.

CHARLES. Thank you. You are always ready with a lecture, arnt you?

LA TRÉMOUILLE [*roughly*] Enough grumbling. What have you got there?

CHARLES. What is that to you?

LA TRÉMOUILLE. It is my business to know what is passing between you and the garrison at Vaucouleurs. [*He snatches*

*the paper from the Dauphin's hand, and begins reading it
with some difficulty, following the words with his finger and
spelling them out syllable by syllable].*

CHARLES [*mortified*] You all think you can treat me as you
please because I owe you money, and because I am no good
at fighting. But I have the blood royal in my veins.

THE ARCHBISHOP. Even that has been questioned, your Highness. One hardly recognizes in you the grandson of Charles
the Wise.

CHARLES. I want to hear no more of my grandfather. He was
so wise that he used up the whole family stock of wisdom for
five generations, and left me the poor fool I am, bullied and
insulted by all of you.

THE ARCHBISHOP. Control yourself, sir. These outbursts of
petulance are not seemly.

CHARLES. Another lecture! Thank you. What a pity it is that
though you are an archbishop saints and angels dont come to
see you!

THE ARCHBISHOP. What do you mean?

CHARLES. Aha! Ask that bully there [*pointing to La Trémouille*].

LA TRÉMOUILLE [*furious*] Hold your tongue. Do you hear?

CHARLES. Oh, I hear. You neednt shout. The whole castle can
hear. Why dont you go and shout at the English, and beat
them for me?

LA TRÉMOUILLE [*raising his fist*] You young –

CHARLES [*running behind the Archbishop*] Dont you raise your
hand to me. It's high treason.

LA HIRE. Steady, Duke! Steady!

THE ARCHBISHOP [*resolutely*] Come, come! this will not do.
My Lord Chamberlain: please! please! we must keep some
sort of order. [*To the Dauphin*] And you, sir: if you cannot
rule your kingdom, at least try to rule yourself.

CHARLES. Another lecture! Thank you.

LA TRÉMOUILLE [*handing over the paper to the Archbishop*]
Here: read the accursed thing for me. He has sent the blood
boiling into my head: I cant distinguish the letters.

CHARLES [*coming back and peering round La Trémouille's left*

shoulder] I will read it for you if you like. I c a n read, you
know.

LA TRÉMOUILLE [*with intense contempt, not at all stung by
the taunt*] Yes: reading is about all you are fit for. Can you
make it out, Archbishop?

THE ARCHBISHOP. I should have expected more commonsense
from De Baudricourt. He is sending some cracked country
lass here –

CHARLES [*interrupting*] No: he is sending a saint: an angel.
And she is coming to me: to m e , the king, and not to you,
Archbishop, holy as you are. She knows the blood royal if
you dont. [*He struts up to the curtains between Bluebeard
and La Hire*].

THE ARCHBISHOP. You cannot be allowed to see this crazy
wench.

CHARLES [*turning*] But I am the king; and I will.

LA TRÉMOUILLE [*brutally*] Then she cannot be allowed to see
y o u . Now!

CHARLES. I tell you I will. I am going to put my foot down –

BLUEBEARD [*laughing at him*] Naughty! What would your
wise grandfather say?

CHARLES. That just shews your ignorance, Bluebeard. My
grandfather had a saint who used to float in the air when she
was praying, and told him everything he wanted to know. My
poor father had two saints, Marie de Maillé and the Gasque
of Avignon. It is in our family; and I dont care what you say:
I will have my saint too.

THE ARCHBISHOP. This creature is not a saint. She is not even
a respectable woman. She does not wear women's clothes.
She is dressed like a soldier, and rides round the country with
soldiers. Do you suppose such a person can be admitted to
your Highness's court?

LA HIRE. Stop. [*Going to the Archbishop*] Did you say a girl in
armor, like a soldier?

THE ARCHBISHOP. So De Baudricourt describes her.

LA HIRE. But by all the devils in hell – Oh, God forgive me, what
am I saying? – by Our Lady and all the saints, this must be the
angel that struck Foul Mouthed Frank dead for swearing.

CHARLES [*triumphant*] You see! A miracle!

LA HIRE. She may strike the lot of us dead if we cross her. For Heaven's sake, Archbishop, be careful what you are doing.

THE ARCHBISHOP [*severely*] Rubbish! Nobody has been struck dead. A drunken blackguard who has been rebuked a hundred times for swearing has fallen into a well, and been drowned. A mere coincidence.

LA HIRE. I do not know what a coincidence is. I do know that the man is dead, and that she told him he was going to die.

THE ARCHBISHOP. We are all going to die, Captain.

LA HIRE [*crossing himself*] I hope not. [*He backs out of the conversation*].

BLUEBEARD. We can easily find out whether she is an angel or not. Let us arrange when she comes that I shall be the Dauphin, and see whether she will find me out.

CHARLES. Yes: I agree to that. If she cannot find the blood royal I will have nothing to do with her.

THE ARCHBISHOP. It is for the Church to make saints: let De Baudricourt mind his own business, and not dare usurp the function of his priest. I say the girl shall not be admitted.

BLUEBEARD. But, Archbishop –

THE ARCHBISHOP [*sternly*] I speak in the Church's name. [*To the Dauphin*] Do you dare say she shall?

CHARLES [*intimidated but sulky*] Oh, if you make it an excommunication matter, I have nothing more to say, of course. But you havnt read the end of the letter. De Baudricourt says she will raise the siege of Orleans, and beat the English for us.

LA TRÉMOUILLE. Rot!

CHARLES. Well, will y o u save Orleans for us, with all your bullying?

LA TRÉMOUILLE [*savagely*] Do not throw that in my face again: do you hear? I have done more fighting than you ever did or ever will. But I cannot be everywhere.

THE DAUPHIN. Well, thats something.

BLUEBEARD [*coming between the Archbishop and Charles*]

You have Jack Dunois at the head of your troops in Orleans: the brave Dunois, the handsome Dunois, the wonderful invincible Dunois, the darling of all the ladies, the beautiful bastard. Is it likely that the country lass can do what he cannot do?

CHARLES. Why doesnt he raise the siege, then?

LA HIRE. The wind is against him.

BLUEBEARD. How can the wind hurt him at Orleans? It is not on the Channel.

LA HIRE. It is on the river Loire; and the English hold the bridgehead. He must ship his men across the river and upstream, if he is to take them in the rear. Well, he cannot, because there is a devil of a wind blowing the other way. He is tired of paying the priests to pray for a west wind. What he needs is a miracle. You tell me that what the girl did to Foul Mouthed Frank was no miracle. No matter: it finished Frank. If she changes the wind for Dunois, that may not be a miracle either; but it may finish the English. What harm is there in trying?

THE ARCHBISHOP [*who has read the end of the letter and become more thoughtful*] It is true that De Baudricourt seems extraordinarily impressed.

LA HIRE. De Baudricourt is a blazing ass; but he is a soldier; and if he thinks she can beat the English, all the rest of the army will think so too.

LA TRÉMOUILLE [*to the Archbishop, who is hesitating*] Oh, let them have their way. Dunois' men will give up the town in spite of him if somebody does not put some fresh spunk into them.

THE ARCHBISHOP. The Church must examine the girl before anything decisive is done about her. However, since his Highness desires it, let her attend the Court.

LA HIRE. I will find her and tell her. [*He goes out*].

CHARLES. Come with me, Bluebeard; and let us arrange so that she will not know who I am. You will pretend to be me. [*He goes out through the curtains*].

BLUEBEARD. Pretend to be that thing! Holy Michael! [*He follows the Dauphin*].

LA TRÉMOUILLE. I wonder will she pick him out!

THE ARCHBISHOP. Of course she will.

LA TRÉMOUILLE. Why? How is she to know?

THE ARCHBISHOP. She will know what everybody in Chinon knows: that the Dauphin is the meanest-looking and worst-dressed figure in the Court, and that the man with the blue beard is Gilles de Rais.

LA TRÉMOUILLE. I never thought of that.

THE ARCHBISHOP. You are not so accustomed to miracles as I am. It is part of my profession.

LA TRÉMOUILLE [*puzzled and a little scandalized*] But that would not be a miracle at all.

THE ARCHBISHOP [*calmly*] Why not?

LA TRÉMOUILLE. Well, come! what is a miracle?

THE ARCHBISHOP. A miracle, my friend, is an event which creates faith. That is the purpose and nature of miracles. They may seem very wonderful to the people who witness them, and very simple to those who perform them. That does not matter: if they confirm or create faith they are true miracles.

LA TRÉMOUILLE. Even when they are frauds, do you mean?

THE ARCHBISHOP. Frauds deceive. An event which creates faith does not deceive: therefore it is not a fraud, but a miracle.

LA TRÉMOUILLE [*scratching his neck in his perplexity*] Well, I suppose as you are an archbishop you must be right. It seems a bit fishy to me. But I am no churchman, and dont understand these matters.

THE ARCHBISHOP. You are not a churchman; but you are a diplomatist and a soldier. Could you make our citizens pay war taxes, or our soldiers sacrifice their lives, if they knew what is really happening instead of what seems to them to be happening?

LA TRÉMOUILLE. No, by Saint Dennis: the fat would be in the fire before sundown.

THE ARCHBISHOP. Would it not be quite easy to tell them the truth?

LA TRÉMOUILLE. Man alive, they wouldnt believe it.

THE ARCHBISHOP. Just so. Well, the Church has to rule men for the good of their souls as you have to rule them for the good of their bodies. To do that, the Church must do as you do: nourish their faith by poetry.

LA TRÉMOUILLE. Poetry! I should call it humbug.

THE ARCHBISHOP. You would be wrong, my friend. Parables are not lies because they describe events that have never happened. Miracles are not frauds because they are often – I do not say always – very simple and innocent contrivances by which the priest fortifies the faith of his flock. When this girl picks out the Dauphin among his courtiers, it will not be a miracle for me, because I shall know how it has been done, and my faith will not be increased. But as for the others, if they feel the thrill of the supernatural, and forget their sinful clay in a sudden sense of the glory of God, it will be a miracle and a blessed one. And you will find that the girl herself will be more affected than anyone else. She will forget how she really picked him out. So, perhaps, will you.

LA TRÉMOUILLE. Well, I wish I were clever enough to know how much of you is God's archbishop and how much the most artful fox in Touraine. Come on, or we shall be late for the fun; and I want to see it, miracle or no miracle.

THE ARCHBISHOP [detaining him a moment] Do not think that I am a lover of crooked ways. There is a new spirit rising in men: we are at the dawning of a wider epoch. If I were a simple monk, and had not to rule men, I should seek peace for my spirit with Aristotle and Pythagoras rather than with the saints and their miracles.

LA TRÉMOUILLE. And who the deuce was Pythagoras?

THE ARCHBISHOP. A sage who held that the earth is round, and that it moves round the sun.

LA TRÉMOUILLE. What an utter fool! Couldnt he use his eyes?

They go out together through the curtains, which are presently withdrawn, revealing the full depth of the throne room with the Court assembled. On the right are two Chairs of State on a dais. Bluebeard is standing theatrically on the dais, playing the king, and, like the courtiers, enjoying the joke rather obviously. There is a curtained arch in the wall behind the dais; but the main door, guarded by men-at-arms, is at

*the other side of the room; and a clear path across is kept and
lined by the courtiers. Charles is in this path in the middle of
the room. La Hire is on his right. The Archbishop, on his left,
has taken his place by the dais: La Trémouille at the other
side of it. The Duchess de la Trémouille, pretending to be the
Queen, sits in the Consort's chair, with a group of ladies in
waiting close by, behind the Archbishop.*

*The chatter of the courtiers makes such a noise that nobody
notices the appearance of the page at the door.*

THE PAGE. The Duke of – [*Nobody listens*]. The Duke of – [*The
chatter continues. Indignant at his failure to command a
hearing, he snatches the halberd of the nearest man-at-arms,
and thumps the floor with it. The chatter ceases; and everybody looks at him in silence*]. Attention! [*He restores the
halberd to the man-at-arms*]. The Duke of Vendôme presents
Joan the Maid to his Majesty.

CHARLES [*putting his finger on his lip*] Ssh! [*He hides behind
the nearest courtier, peering out to see what happens*].

BLUEBEARD [*majestically*] Let her approach the throne.

*Joan, dressed as a soldier, with her hair bobbed and hanging
thickly round her face, is led in by a bashful and speechless
nobleman, from whom she detaches herself to stop and look
around eagerly for the Dauphin.*

THE DUCHESS [*to the nearest lady in waiting*] My dear! Her
hair.

All the ladies explode in uncontrollable laughter.

BLUEBEARD [*trying not to laugh, and waving his hand in
deprecation of their merriment*] Ssh – ssh! Ladies! Ladies!!

JOAN [*not at all embarrassed*] I wear it like this because I am a
soldier. Where be Dauphin?

A titter runs through the Court as she walks to the dais.

BLUEBEARD [*condescendingly*] You are in the presence of the
Dauphin.

*Joan looks at him sceptically for a moment, scanning him
hard up and down to make sure. Dead silence, all watching
her. Fun dawns in her face.*

JOAN. Coom, Bluebeard! Thou canst not fool me. Where be
Dauphin?

*A roar of laughter breaks out as Gilles, with a gesture of
surrender, joins in the laugh, and jumps down from the dais
beside La Trémouille. Joan, also on the broad grin, turns
back, searching along the row of courtiers, and presently
makes a dive, and drags out Charles by the arm.*

JOAN [*releasing him and bobbing him a little curtsey*] Gentle
little Dauphin, I am sent to you to drive the English away
from Orleans and from France, and to crown you king in
the cathedral at Rheims, where all true kings of France are
crowned.

CHARLES [*triumphant, to the Court*] You see, all of you; she
knew the blood royal. Who dare say now that I am not my
father's son? [*To Joan*] But if you want me to be crowned at
Rheims you must talk to the Archbishop, not to me. There he
is [*he is standing behind her*]!

JOAN [*turning quickly, overwhelmed with emotion*] Oh, my
lord! [*She falls on both knees before him, with bowed head,
not daring to look up*] My lord: I am only a poor country girl;
and you are filled with the blessedness and glory of God
Himself; but you will touch me with your hands, and give me
your blessing, wont you?

BLUEBEARD [*whispering to La Trémouille*] The old fox
blushes.

LA TRÉMOUILLE. Another miracle!

THE ARCHBISHOP [*touched, putting his hand on her head*]
Child: you are in love with religion.

JOAN [*startled: looking up at him*] Am I? I never thought of
that. Is there any harm in it?

THE ARCHBISHOP. There is no harm in it, my child. But there
is danger.

JOAN [*rising, with a sunflush of reckless happiness irradiating
her face*] There is always danger, except in heaven. Oh, my
lord, you have given me such strength, such courage. It must
be a most wonderful thing to be Archbishop.

The Court smiles broadly: even titters a little.

THE ARCHBISHOP [*drawing himself up sensitively*] Gentlemen:
your levity is rebuked by this maid's faith. I am, God help me,
all unworthy; but your mirth is a deadly sin.

Their faces fall. Dead silence.

BLUEBEARD. My lord: we were laughing at her, not at you.

THE ARCHBISHOP. What? Not at my unworthiness but at her faith! Gilles de Rais: this maid prophesied that the blasphemer should be drowned in his sin –

JOAN [*distressed*] No!

THE ARCHBISHOP [*silencing her by a gesture*] I prophesy now that you will be hanged in yours if you do not learn when to laugh and when to pray.

BLUEBEARD. My lord: I stand rebuked. I am sorry: I can say no more. But if you prophesy that I shall be hanged, I shall never be able to resist temptation, because I shall always be telling myself that I may as well be hanged for a sheep as a lamb.

The courtiers take heart at this. There is more tittering.

JOAN [*scandalized*] You are an idle fellow, Bluebeard; and you have great impudence to answer the Archbishop.

LA HIRE [*with a huge chuckle*] Well said, lass! Well said!

JOAN [*impatiently to the Archbishop*] Oh, my lord, will you send all these silly folks away so that I may speak to the Dauphin alone?

LA HIRE [*goodhumoredly*] I can take a hint. [*He salutes; turns on his heel; and goes out*].

THE ARCHBISHOP. Come, gentlemen. The Maid comes with God's blessing, and must be obeyed.

The courtiers withdraw, some through the arch, others at the opposite side. The Archbishop marches across to the door, followed by the Duchess and La Trémouille. As the Archbishop passes Joan, she falls on her knees, and kisses the hem of his robe fervently. He shakes his head in instinctive remonstrance; gathers the robe from her; and goes out. She is left kneeling directly in the Duchess's way.

THE DUCHESS [*coldly*] Will you allow me to pass, please?

JOAN [*hastily rising, and standing back*] Beg pardon, maam, I am sure.

The Duchess passes on. Joan stares after her; then whispers to the Dauphin.

JOAN. Be that Queen?

CHARLES. No. She thinks she is.

JOAN [*again staring after the Duchess*] Oo-oo-ooh! [*Her awe-struck amazement at the figure cut by the magnificently dressed lady is not wholly complimentary*].

LA TRÉMOUILLE [*very surly*] I'll trouble your Highness not to gibe at my wife. [*He goes out. The others have already gone*].

JOAN [*to the Dauphin*] Who be old Gruff-and-Grum?

CHARLES. He is the Duke de la Trémouille.

JOAN. What be his job?

CHARLES. He pretends to command the army. And whenever I find a friend I can care for, he kills him.

JOAN. Why dost let him?

CHARLES [*petulantly moving to the throne side of the room to escape from her magnetic field*] How can I prevent him? He bullies me. They all bully me.

JOAN. Art afraid?

CHARLES. Yes: I am afraid. It's no use preaching to me about it. It's all very well for these big men with their armor that is too heavy for me, and their swords that I can hardly lift, and their muscle and their shouting and their bad tempers. They like fighting: most of them are making fools of themselves all the time they are not fighting; but I am quiet and sensible; and I dont want to kill people: I only want to be left alone to enjoy myself in my own way. I never asked to be a king: it was pushed on me. So if you are going to say 'Son of St Louis: gird on the sword of your ancestors, and lead us to victory' you may spare your breath to cool your porridge; for I cannot do it. I am not built that way; and there is an end of it.

JOAN [*trenchant and masterful*] Blethers! We are all like that to begin with. I shall put courage into thee.

CHARLES. But I dont want to have courage put into me. I want to sleep in a comfortable bed, and not live in continual terror of being killed or wounded. Put courage into the others, and let them have their bellyful of fighting; but let me alone.

JOAN. It's no use, Charlie: thou must face what God puts on thee. If thou fail to make thyself king, thoult be a beggar: what else art fit for? Come! Let me see thee sitting on the throne. I have looked forward to that.

CHARLES. What is the good of sitting on the throne when the other fellows give all the orders? However! [*he sits enthroned, a piteous figure*] here is the king for you! Look your fill at the poor devil.

JOAN. Thourt not king yet, lad: thourt but Dauphin. Be not led away by them around thee. Dressing up dont fill empty noddle. I know the people: the real people that make thy bread for thee; and I tell thee they count no man king of France until the holy oil has been poured on his hair, and himself consecrated and crowned in Rheims Cathedral. And thou needs new clothes, Charlie. Why does not Queen look after thee properly?

CHARLES. We're too poor. She wants all the money we can spare to put on her own back. Besides, I like to see her beautifully dressed; and I dont care what I wear myself: I should look ugly anyhow.

JOAN. There is some good in thee, Charlie; but it is not yet a king's good.

CHARLES. We shall see. I am not such a fool as I look. I have my eyes open; and I can tell you that one good treaty is worth ten good fights. These fighting fellows lose all on the treaties that they gain on the fights. If we can only have a treaty, the English are sure to have the worst of it, because they are better at fighting than at thinking.

JOAN. If the English win, it is they that will make the treaty; and then God help poor France! Thou must fight, Charlie, whether thou will or no. I will go first to hearten thee. We must take our courage in both hands: aye, and pray for it with both hands too.

CHARLES [*descending from his throne and again crossing the room to escape from her dominating urgency*] Oh do stop talking about God and praying. I cant bear people who are always praying. Isnt it bad enough to have to do it at the proper times?

JOAN [*pitying him*] Thou poor child, thou hast never prayed in thy life. I must teach thee from the beginning.

CHARLES. I am not a child: I am a grown man and a father; and I will not be taught any more.

JOAN. Aye, you have a little son. He that will be Louis the
Eleventh when you die. Would you not fight for him?

CHARLES. No: a horrid boy. He hates me. He hates everybody,
selfish little beast! I dont want to be bothered with children. I
dont want to be a father; and I dont want to be a son: especially
a son of St Louis. I dont want to be any of these fine things
you all have your heads full of: I want to be just what I am.
Why cant you mind your own business, and let me mind
mine?

JOAN [again contemptuous] Minding your own business is like
minding your own body: it's the shortest way to make yourself
sick. What is my business? Helping mother at home. What is
thine? Petting lapdogs and sucking sugar-sticks. I call that
muck. I tell thee it is God's business we are here to do: not
our own. I have a message to thee from God; and thou must
listen to it, though thy heart break with the terror of it.

CHARLES. I dont want a message; but can you tell me any
secrets? Can you do any cures? Can you turn lead into gold,
or anything of that sort?

JOAN. I can turn thee into a king, in Rheims Cathedral; and
that is a miracle that will take some doing, it seems.

CHARLES. If we go to Rheims, and have a coronation, Anne
will want new dresses. We cant afford them. I am all right as
I am.

JOAN. As you are! And what is that? Less than my father's
poorest shepherd. Thourt not lawful owner of thy own land
of France till thou be consecrated.

CHARLES. But I shall not be lawful owner of my own land
anyhow. Will the consecration pay off my mortgages? I have
pledged my last acre to the Archbishop and that fat bully. I
owe money even to Bluebeard.

JOAN [earnestly] Charlie: I come from the land, and have gotten
my strength working on the land; and I tell thee that the land
is thine to rule righteously and keep God's peace in, and not
to pledge at the pawnshop as a drunken woman pledges her
children's clothes. And I come from God to tell thee to kneel
in the cathedral and solemnly give thy kingdom to Him for
ever and ever, and become the greatest king in the world as

His steward and His bailiff, His soldier and His servant. The very clay of France will become holy: her soldiers will be the soldiers of God: the rebel dukes will be rebels against God: the English will fall on their knees and beg thee let them return to their lawful homes in peace. Wilt be a poor little Judas, and betray me and Him that sent me?

CHARLES [*tempted at last*] Oh, if I only dare!

JOAN. I shall dare, dare, and dare again, in God's name! Art for or against me?

CHARLES [*excited*] I'll risk it, I warn you I shant be able to keep it up; but I'll risk it. You shall see. [*Running to the main door and shouting*] Hallo! Come back, everybody. [*To Joan, as he runs back to the arch opposite*] Mind you stand by and dont let me be bullied. [*Through the arch*] Come along, will you: the whole Court. [*He sits down in the royal chair as they all hurry in to their former places, chattering and wondering*]. Now I'm in for it; but no matter: here goes! [*To the page*] Call for silence, you little beast, will you?

THE PAGE [*snatching a halberd as before and thumping with it repeatedly*] Silence for His Majesty the King. The King speaks. [*Peremptorily*] Will you be silent there? [*Silence*].

CHARLES [*rising*] I have given the command of the army to The Maid. The Maid is to do as she likes with it. [*He descends from the dais*].

   General amazement. La Hire, delighted, slaps his steel thigh-piece with his gauntlet.

LA TRÉMOUILLE [*turning threateningly towards Charles*] What is this? *I* command the army.

   Joan quickly puts her hand on Charles's shoulder as he instinctively recoils. Charles, with a grotesque effort culminating in an extravagant gesture, snaps his fingers in the Chamberlain's face.

JOAN. Thourt answered, old Gruff-and-Grum. [*Suddenly flashing out her sword as she divines that her moment has come*] Who is for God and His Maid? Who is for Orleans with me?

LA HIRE [*carried away, drawing also*] For God and His Maid! To Orleans!

ALL THE KNIGHTS [*following his lead with enthusiasm*] To
Orleans!

Joan, radiant, falls on her knees in thanksgiving to God.
They all kneel, except the Archbishop, who gives his benedic-
tion with a sigh, and La Trémouille, who collapses, cursing.

corruption
in Church

SCENE III

Dunois' character development (handwritten annotation)

Orleans, 29th April 1429. Dunois, aged 26, is pacing up and down a patch of ground on the south bank of the silver Loire, commanding a long view of the river in both directions. He has had his lance stuck up with a pennon, which streams in a strong east wind. His shield with its bend sinister lies beside it. He has his commander's baton in his hand. He is well built, carrying his armor easily. His broad brow and pointed chin give him an equilaterally triangular face, already marked by active service and responsibility, with the expression of a goodnatured and capable man who has no affectations and no foolish illusions. His page is sitting on the ground, elbows on knees, cheeks on fists, idly watching the water. It is evening; and both man and boy are affected by the loveliness of the Loire.

DUNOIS [*halting for a moment to glance up at the streaming pennon and shake his head wearily before he resumes his pacing*] West wind, west wind, west wind. Strumpet: steadfast when you should be wanton, wanton when you should be steadfast. West wind on the silver Loire: what rhymes to Loire? [*He looks again at the pennon, and shakes his fist at it*] Change, curse you, change, English harlot of a wind, change. West, west, I tell you. [*With a growl he resumes his march in silence, but soon begins again*] West wind, wanton wind, wilful wind, womanish wind, false wind from over the water, will you never blow again? *(alliteration — handwritten annotation)*

THE PAGE [*bounding to his feet*] See! There! There she goes!

DUNOIS [*startled from his reverie: eagerly*] Where? Who? The Maid?

THE PAGE. No: the kingfisher. Like blue lightning. She went into that bush.

DUNOIS [*furiously disappointed*] Is that all? You infernal young idiot: I have a mind to pitch you into the river.

THE PAGE [*not afraid, knowing his man*] It looked frightfully jolly, that flash of blue. Look! There goes the other!

DUNOIS [*running eagerly to the river brim*] Where? Where?

THE PAGE [*pointing*] Passing the reeds.

DUNOIS [*delighted*] I see.

> *They follow the flight till the bird takes cover.*

THE PAGE. You blew me up because you were not in time to see them yesterday.

DUNOIS. You knew I was expecting The Maid when you set up your yelping. I will give you something to yelp for next time.

THE PAGE. Arnt they lovely? I wish I could catch them.

DUNOIS. Let me catch you trying to trap them, and I will put you in the iron cage for a month to teach you what a cage feels like. You are an abominable boy.

> *The page laughs, and squats down as before.*

DUNOIS [*pacing*] Blue bird, blue bird, since I am friend to thee, change thou the wind for me. No: it does not rhyme. He who has sinned for thee: thats better. No sense in it, though. [*He finds himself close to the page*] You abominable boy! [*He turns away from him*] Mary in the blue snood, kingfisher color: will you grudge me a west wind?

A SENTRY'S VOICE WESTWARD. Halt! Who goes there?

JOAN'S VOICE. The Maid.

DUNOIS. Let her pass. Hither, Maid! To me!

> *Joan, in splendid armor, rushes in in a blazing rage. The wind drops; and the pennon flaps idly down the lance; but Dunois is too much occupied with Joan to notice it.*

JOAN [*bluntly*] Be you Bastard of Orleans?

DUNOIS [*cool and stern, pointing to his shield*] You see the bend sinister. Are you Joan the Maid?

JOAN. Sure.

DUNOIS. Where are your troops?

JOAN. Miles behind. They have cheated me. They have brought me to the wrong side of the river.

DUNOIS. I told them to.

JOAN. Why did you? The English are on the other side!

DUNOIS. The English are on both sides.

JOAN. But Orleans is on the other side. We must fight the English there. How can we cross the river?

DUNOIS [*grimly*] There is a bridge.

relaxed relationship

JOAN. In God's name, then, let us cross the bridge, and fall on them.

DUNOIS. It seems simple; but it cannot be done.

JOAN. Who says so?

DUNOIS. I say so; and older and wiser heads than mine are of the same opinion.

JOAN [*roundly*] Then you older and wiser heads are fat-heads: they have made a fool of you; and now they want to make a fool of me too, bringing me to the wrong side of the river. Do you not know that I bring you better help than ever came to any general or any town?

DUNOIS [*smiling patiently*] Your own?

JOAN. No: the help and counsel of the King of Heaven. Which is the way to the bridge?

DUNOIS. You are impatient, Maid.

JOAN. Is this a time for patience? Our enemy is at our gates; and here we stand doing nothing. Oh, why are you not fighting? Listen to me: I will deliver you from fear. I –

DUNOIS [*laughing heartily, and waving her off*] No, no, my girl: if you delivered me from fear I should be a good knight for a story book, but a very bad commander of the army. Come! let me begin to make a soldier of you. [*He takes her to the water's edge*]. Do you see those two forts at this end of the bridge? the big ones?

JOAN. Yes. Are they ours or the goddams'?

DUNOIS. Be quiet, and listen to me. If I were in either of those forts with only ten men I could hold it against an army. The English have more than ten times ten goddams in those forts to hold them against us.

JOAN. They cannot hold them against God. God did not give them the land under those forts: they stole it from Him. He gave it to us. I will take those forts.

DUNOIS. Single-handed?

JOAN. Our men will take them. I will lead them.

DUNOIS. Not a man will follow you.

JOAN. I will not look back to see whether anyone is following me.

DUNOIS [*recognizing her mettle, and clapping her heartily on*

the shoulder] Good. You have the makings of a soldier in
you. You are in love with war.

JOAN [*startled*] Oh! And the Archbishop said I was in love with
religion.

DUNOIS. I, God forgive me, am a little in love with war myself,
the ugly devil! I am like a man with two wives. Do you want
to be like a woman with two husbands?

JOAN [*matter-of-fact*] I will never take a husband. A man in
Toul took an action against me for breach of promise; but I
never promised him. I am a soldier: I do not want to be
thought of as a woman. I will not dress as a woman. I do not
care for the things women care for. They dream of lovers, and
of money. I dream of leading a charge, and of placing the big
guns. You soldiers do not know how to use the big guns: you
think you can win battles with a great noise and smoke.

DUNOIS [*with a shrug*] True. Half the time the artillery is more
trouble than it is worth.

JOAN. Aye, lad; but you cannot fight stone walls with horses:
you must have guns, and much bigger guns too.

DUNOIS [*grinning at her familiarity, and echoing it*] Aye, lass;
but a good heart and a stout ladder will get over the stoniest
wall.

JOAN. I will be first up the ladder when we reach the fort,
Bastard. I dare you to follow me.

DUNOIS. You must not dare a staff officer, Joan: only company
officers are allowed to indulge in displays of personal courage.
Besides, you must know that I welcome you as a saint, not as
a soldier. I have daredevils enough at my call, if they could
help me.

JOAN. I am not a daredevil: I am a servant of God. My sword
is sacred: I found it behind the altar in the church of
St Catherine, where God hid it for me; and I may not strike a
blow with it. My heart is full of courage, not of anger. I will
lead; and your men will follow: that is all I can do. But I must
do it: you shall not stop me.

DUNOIS. All in good time. Our men cannot take those forts by
a sally across the bridge. They must come by water, and take
the English in the rear on this side.

JOAN [*her military sense asserting itself*] Then make rafts and put big guns on them; and let your men cross to us.

DUNOIS. The rafts are ready; and the men are embarked. But they must wait for God.

JOAN. What do you mean? God is waiting for them.

DUNOIS. Let Him send us a wind then. My boats are downstream: they cannot come up against both wind and current. We must wait until God changes the wind. Come: let me take you to the church.

JOAN. No. I love church; but the English will not yield to prayers: they understand nothing but hard knocks and slashes. I will not go to church until we have beaten them.

DUNOIS. You must: I have business for you there.

JOAN. What business?

DUNOIS. To pray for a west wind. I have prayed; and I have given two silver candlesticks; but my prayers are not answered. Yours may be: you are young and innocent.

JOAN. Oh yes: you are right. I will pray: I will tell St Catherine: she will make God give me a west wind. Quick: shew me the way to the church.

THE PAGE [*sneezes violently*] At-cha!!!

JOAN. God bless you, child! Coom, Bastard.

> *They go out. The page rises to follow. He picks up the shield, and is taking the spear as well when he notices the pennon, which is now streaming eastward.*

THE PAGE [*dropping the shield and calling excitedly after them*] Seigneur! Seigneur! Mademoiselle!

DUNOIS [*running back*] What is it? The kingfisher? [*He looks eagerly for it up the river*].

JOAN [*joining them*] Oh, a kingfisher! Where?

THE PAGE. No: the wind, the wind, the wind [*pointing to the pennon*]: that is what made me sneeze.

DUNOIS [*looking at the pennon*] The wind has changed. [*He crosses himself*] God has spoken. [*Kneeling and handing his baton to Joan*] You command the king's army. I am your soldier.

THE PAGE [*looking down the river*] The boats have put off. They are ripping upstream like anything.

DUNOIS [*rising*] Now for the forts. You dared me to follow. Dare you lead?

JOAN [*bursting into tears and flinging her arms round Dunois, kissing him on both cheeks*] Dunois, dear comrade in arms, help me. My eyes are blinded with tears. Set my foot on the ladder, and say 'Up, Joan.'

DUNOIS [*dragging her out*] Never mind the tears: make for the flash of the guns.

JOAN [*in a blaze of courage*] Ah!

DUNOIS [*dragging her along with him*] For God and Saint Dennis!

THE PAGE [*shrilly*] The Maid! The Maid! God and The Maid! Hurray-ay-ay! [*He snatches up the shield and lance, and capers out after them, mad with excitement*].

1st scene of English folk
SCENE IV

A tent in the English camp. A bullnecked English chaplain of 50 is sitting on a stool at a table, hard at work writing. At the other side of the table an imposing nobleman, aged 46, is seated in a handsome chair turning over the leaves of an illuminated Book of Hours. The nobleman is enjoying himself: the chaplain is struggling with suppressed wrath. There is an unoccupied leather stool on the nobleman's left. The table is on his right.

THE NOBLEMAN. Now this is what I call workmanship. There is nothing on earth more exquisite than a bonny book, with well-placed columns of rich black writing in beautiful borders, and illuminated pictures cunningly inset. But nowadays, instead of looking at books, people read them. A book might as well be one of those orders for bacon and bran that you are scribbling.

THE CHAPLAIN. I must say, my lord, you take our situation very coolly. Very coolly indeed.

THE NOBLEMAN [*supercilious*] What is the matter?

THE CHAPLAIN. The matter, my lord, is that we English have been defeated.

THE NOBLEMAN. That happens, you know. It is only in history books and ballads that the enemy is always defeated.

THE CHAPLAIN. But we are being defeated over and over again. First, Orleans –

THE NOBLEMAN [*poohpoohing*] Oh, Orleans!

THE CHAPLAIN. I know what you are going to say, my lord: that was a clear case of witchcraft and sorcery. But we are still being defeated. Jargeau, Meung, Beaugency, just like Orleans. And now we have been butchered at Patay, and Sir John Talbot taken prisoner. [*He throws down his pen, almost in tears*] I feel it, my lord: I feel it very deeply. I cannot bear to see my countrymen defeated by a parcel of foreigners.

THE NOBLEMAN. Oh! you are an Englishman, are you?

THE CHAPLAIN. Certainly not, my lord: I am a gentleman. Still, like your lordship, I was born in England; and it makes a difference.

THE NOBLEMAN. You are attached to the soil, eh?

THE CHAPLAIN. It pleases your lordship to be satirical at my expense: your greatness privileges you to be so with impunity. But your lordship knows very well that I am not attached to the soil in a vulgar manner, like a serf. Still, I have a feeling about it; [*with growing agitation*] and I am not ashamed of it; and [*rising wildly*] by God, if this goes on any longer I will fling my cassock to the devil, and take arms myself, and strangle the accursed witch with my own hands.

THE NOBLEMAN [*laughing at him goodnaturedly*] So you shall, chaplain: so you shall, if we can do nothing better. But not yet, not quite yet.

The Chaplain resumes his seat very sulkily.

THE NOBLEMAN [*airily*] I should not care very much about the witch – you see, I have made my pilgrimage to the Holy Land; and the Heavenly Powers, for their own credit, can hardly allow me to be worsted by a village sorceress – but the Bastard of Orleans is a harder nut to crack; and as he has been to the Holy Land too, honors are easy between us as far as that goes.

THE CHAPLAIN. He is only a Frenchman, my lord.

THE NOBLEMAN. A Frenchman! Where did you pick up that expression? Are these Burgundians and Bretons and Picards and Gascons beginning to call themselves Frenchmen, just as our fellows are beginning to call themselves Englishmen? They actually talk of France and England as their countries. Theirs, if you please! What is to become of me and you if that way of thinking comes into fashion?

THE CHAPLAIN. Why, my lord? Can it hurt us?

THE NOBLEMAN. Men cannot serve two masters. If this cant of serving their country once takes hold of them, goodbye to the authority of their feudal lords, and goodbye to the authority of the Church. That is, goodbye to you and me.

THE CHAPLAIN. I hope I am a faithful servant of the Church; and there are only six cousins between me and the barony of Stogumber, which was created by the Conqueror. But is that any reason why I should stand by and see Englishmen beaten by a French bastard and a witch from Lousy Champagne?

THE NOBLEMAN. Easy, man, easy: we shall burn the witch and beat the bastard all in good time. Indeed I am waiting at present for the Bishop of Beauvais, to arrange the burning with him. He has been turned out of his diocese by her faction.

THE CHAPLAIN. You have first to catch her, my lord.

THE NOBLEMAN. Or buy her. I will offer a king's ransom.

THE CHAPLAIN. A king's ransom! For that slut! — low class, slob

THE NOBLEMAN. One has to leave a margin. Some of Charles's people will sell her to the Burgundians; the Burgundians will sell her to us; and there will probably be three or four middlemen who will expect their little commissions.

THE CHAPLAIN. Monstrous. It is all those scoundrels of Jews: they get in every time money changes hands. I would not leave a Jew alive in Christendom if I had my way.

THE NOBLEMAN. Why not? The Jews generally give value. They make you pay; but they deliver the goods. In my experience the men who want something for nothing are invariably Christians.

A page appears.

THE PAGE. The Right Reverend the Bishop of Beauvais: Monseigneur Cauchon.

Cauchon, aged about 60, comes in. The page withdraws. The two Englishmen rise.

THE NOBLEMAN [*with effusive courtesy*] My dear Bishop, how good of you to come! Allow me to introduce myself: Richard de Beauchamp, Earl of Warwick, at your service.

CAUCHON. Your lordship's fame is well known to me.

WARWICK. This reverend cleric is Master John de Stogumber.

THE CHAPLAIN [*glibly*] John Bowyer Spenser Neville de Stogumber, at your service, my lord: Bachelor of Theology, and Keeper of the Private Seal to His Eminence the Cardinal of Winchester.

WARWICK [*to Cauchon*] You call him the Cardinal of England, I believe. Our king's uncle.

CAUCHON. Messire John de Stogumber: I am always the very

good friend of His Eminence. [*He extends his hand to the chaplain, who kisses his ring*].

WARWICK. Do me the honor to be seated. [*He gives Cauchon his chair, placing it at the head of the table*].

Cauchon accepts the place of honor with a grave inclination. Warwick fetches the leather stool carelessly, and sits in his former place. The chaplain goes back to his chair.

Though Warwick has taken second place in calculated deference to the Bishop, he assumes the lead in opening the proceedings as a matter of course. He is still cordial and expansive; but there is a new note in his voice which means that he is coming to business.

WARWICK. Well, my Lord Bishop, you find us in one of our unlucky moments. Charles is to be crowned at Rheims, practically by the young woman from Lorraine; and – I must not deceive you, nor flatter your hopes – we cannot prevent it. I suppose it will make a great difference to Charles's position.

CAUCHON. Undoubtedly. It is a masterstroke of The Maid's.

THE CHAPLAIN [*again agitated*] We were not fairly beaten, my lord. No Englishman is ever fairly beaten.

Cauchon raises his eyebrow slightly, then quickly composes his face.

WARWICK. Our friend here takes the view that the young woman is a sorceress. It would, I presume, be the duty of your reverend lordship to denounce her to the Inquisition, and have her burnt for that offence.

CAUCHON. If she were captured in my diocese: yes.

WARWICK [*feeling that they are getting on capitally*] Just so. Now I suppose there can be no reasonable doubt that she is a sorceress.

THE CHAPLAIN. Not the least. An arrant witch.

WARWICK [*gently reproving their interruption*] We are asking for the Bishop's opinion, Messire John.

CAUCHON. We shall have to consider not merely our own opinions here, but the opinions – the prejudices, if you like – of a French court.

WARWICK [*correcting*] A Catholic court, my lord.

CAUCHON. Catholic courts are composed of mortal men, like

other courts, however sacred their function and inspiration may be. And if the men are Frenchmen, as the modern fashion calls them, I am afraid the bare fact that an English army has been defeated by a French one will not convince them that there is any sorcery in the matter.

THE CHAPLAIN. What! Not when the famous Sir John Talbot himself has been defeated and actually taken prisoner by a drab from the ditches of Lorraine!

CAUCHON. Sir John Talbot, we all know, is a fierce and formidable soldier, Messire; but I have yet to learn that he is an able general. And though it pleases you to say that he has been defeated by this girl, some of us may be disposed to give a little of the credit to Dunois.

THE CHAPLAIN [*contemptuously*] The Bastard of Orleans!

CAUCHON. Let me remind –   4 Dunois

WARWICK [*interposing*] I know what you are going to say, my lord. Dunois defeated m e at Montargis.

CAUCHON [*bowing*] I take that as evidence that the Seigneur Dunois is a very able commander indeed.

WARWICK. Your lordship is the flower of courtesy. I admit, on our side, that Talbot is a mere fighting animal, and that it probably served him right to be taken at Patay.

THE CHAPLAIN [*chafing*] My lord: at Orleans this woman had her throat pierced by an English arrow, and was seen to cry like a child from the pain of it. It was a death wound; yet she fought all day; and when our men had repulsed all her attacks like true Englishmen, she walked alone to the wall of our fort with a white banner in her hand; and our men were paralyzed, and could neither shoot nor strike whilst the French fell on them and drove them on to the bridge, which immediately burst into flames and crumbled under them, letting them down into the river, where they were drowned in heaps. Was this your bastard's generalship? or were those flames the flames of hell, conjured up by witchcraft?

WARWICK. You will forgive Messire John's vehemence, my lord; but he has put our case. Dunois is a great captain, we admit; but why could he do nothing until the witch came?

CAUCHON. I do not say that there were no supernatural powers

on her side. But the names on that white banner were not the
names of Satan and Beelzebub, but the blessed names of our
Lord and His holy mother. And your commander who was
drowned – Clahz-da I think you call him –

WARWICK. Glasdale. Sir William Glasdale.

CAUCHON. Glass-dell, thank you. He was no saint; and many
of our people think that he was drowned for his blasphemies
against The Maid.

WARWICK [*beginning to look very dubious*] Well, what are we
to infer from all this, my lord? Has The Maid converted you?

CAUCHON. If she had, my lord, I should have known better
than to have trusted myself here within your grasp.

WARWICK [*blandly deprecating*] Oh! oh! My lord!

CAUCHON. If the devil is making use of this girl – and I believe
he is –

WARWICK [*reassured*] Ah! You hear, Messire John? I knew
your lordship would not fail us. Pardon my interruption.
Proceed.

CAUCHON. If it be so, the devil has longer views than you give
him credit for.

WARWICK. Indeed? In what way? Listen to this, Messire John.

CAUCHON. If the devil wanted to damn a country girl, do you
think so easy a task would cost him the winning of half a
dozen battles? No, my lord: any trumpery imp could do that
much if the girl could be damned at all. The Prince of Darkness
does not condescend to such cheap drudgery. When he strikes,
he strikes at the Catholic Church, whose realm is the whole
spiritual world. When he damns, he damns the souls of the
entire human race. Against that dreadful design The Church
stands ever on guard. And it is as one of the instruments of
that design that I see this girl. She is inspired, but diabolically
inspired.

THE CHAPLAIN. I told you she was a witch.

CAUCHON [*fiercely*] She is not a witch. She is a heretic.

THE CHAPLAIN. What difference does that make?

CAUCHON. You, a priest, ask me that! You English are strangely
blunt in the mind. All these things that you call witchcraft
are capable of a natural explanation. The woman's miracles

would not impose on a rabbit: she does not claim them as miracles herself. What do her victories prove but that she has a better head on her shoulders than your swearing Glass-dells and mad bull Talbots, and that the courage of faith, even though it be a false faith, will always outstay the courage of wrath?

THE CHAPLAIN [*hardly able to believe his ears*] Does your lordship compare Sir John Talbot, three times Governor of Ireland, to a mad bull?!!!

WARWICK. It would not be seemly for you to do so, Messire John, as you are still six removes from a barony. But as I am an earl, and Talbot is only a knight, I may make bold to accept the comparison. [*To the Bishop*] My lord: I wipe the slate as far as the witchcraft goes. None the less, we must burn the woman.

CAUCHON. I cannot burn her. The Church cannot take life. And my first duty is to seek this girl's salvation.

WARWICK. No doubt. But you do burn people occasionally.

CAUCHON. No. When The Church cuts off an obstinate heretic as a dead branch from the tree of life, the heretic is handed over to the secular arm. The Church has no part in what the secular arm may see fit to do.

WARWICK. Precisely. And I shall be the secular arm in this case. Well, my lord, hand over your dead branch; and I will see that the fire is ready for it. If you will answer for The Church's part, I will answer for the secular part.

CAUCHON [*with smouldering anger*] I can answer for nothing. You great lords are too prone to treat The Church as a mere political convenience.

WARWICK [*smiling and propitiatory*] Not in England, I assure you.

CAUCHON. In England more than anywhere else. No, my lord: the soul of this village girl is of equal value with yours or your king's before the throne of God; and my first duty is to save it. I will not suffer your lordship to smile at me as if I were repeating a meaningless form of words, and it were well understood between us that I should betray the girl to you. I am no mere political bishop: my faith is to me what your honor is to you; and if there be a loophole through which this baptized child of God can creep to her salvation, I shall guide her to it.

THE CHAPLAIN [*rising in a fury*] You are a traitor.

CAUCHON [*springing up*] You lie, priest. [*Trembling with rage*] If you dare do what this woman has done – set your country above the holy Catholic Church – you shall go to the fire with her.

THE CHAPLAIN. My lord: I – I went too far. I – [*he sits down with a submissive gesture*].

WARWICK [*who has risen apprehensively*] My lord: I apologize to you for the word used by Messire John de Stogumber. It does not mean in England what it does in France. In your language traitor means betrayer: one who is perfidious, treacherous, unfaithful, disloyal. In our country it means simply one who is not wholly devoted to our English interests.

CAUCHON. I am sorry: I did not understand. [*He subsides into his chair with dignity*].

WARWICK [*resuming his seat, much relieved*] I must apologize on my own account if I have seemed to take the burning of this poor girl too lightly. When one has seen whole country-sides burnt over and over again as mere items in military routine, one has to grow a very thick skin. Otherwise one might go mad: at all events, I should. May I venture to assume that your lordship also, having to see so many heretics burned from time to time, is compelled to take – shall I say a professional view of what would otherwise be a very horrible incident?

CAUCHON. Yes: it is a painful duty: even, as you say, a horrible one. But in comparison with the horror of heresy it is less than nothing. I am not thinking of this girl's body, which will suffer for a few moments only, and which must in any event die in some more or less painful manner, but of her soul, which may suffer to all eternity.

WARWICK. Just so; and God grant that her soul may be saved! But the practical problem would seem to be how to save her soul without saving her body. For we must face it, my lord: if this cult of The Maid goes on, our cause is lost.

THE CHAPLAIN [*his voice broken like that of a man who has been crying*] May I speak, my lord?

WARWICK. Really, Messire John, I had rather you did not, unless you can keep your temper.

THE CHAPLAIN. It is only this. I speak under correction; but The Maid is full of deceit: she pretends to be devout. Her prayers and confessions are endless. How can she be accused of heresy when she neglects no observance of a faithful daughter of The Church?

CAUCHON [*flaming up*] A faithful daughter of The Church! The Pope himself at his proudest dare not presume as this woman presumes. She acts as if she herself were The Church. She brings the message of God to Charles; and The Church must stand aside. She will crown him in the cathedral of Rheims: s h e, not The Church! She sends letters to the king of England giving him God's command through h e r to return to his island on pain of God's vengeance, which s h e will execute. Let me tell you that the writing of such letters was the practice of the accursed Mahomet, the anti-Christ. Has she ever in all her utterances said one word of The Church? Never. It is always God and herself.

WARWICK. What can you expect? A beggar on horseback! Her head is turned.

CAUCHON. Who has turned it? The devil. And for a mighty purpose. He is spreading this heresy everywhere. The man Hus, burnt only thirteen years ago at Constance, infected all Bohemia with it. A man named WcLeef, himself an anointed priest, spread the pestilence in England; and to your shame you let him die in his bed. We have such people here in France too: I know the breed. It is cancerous: if it be not cut out, stamped out, burnt out, it will not stop until it has brought the whole body of human society into sin and corruption, into waste and ruin. By it an Arab camel driver drove Christ and His Church out of Jerusalem, and ravaged his way west like a wild beast until at last there stood only the Pyrenees and God's mercy between France and damnation. Yet what did the camel driver do at the beginning more than this shepherd girl is doing? He had his voices from the

angel Gabriel: she has her voices from St Catherine and
St Margaret and the Blessed Michael. He declared himself the
messenger of God, and wrote in God's name to the kings of
the earth. Her letters to them are going forth daily. It is
not the Mother of God now to whom we must look for
intercession, but to Joan the Maid. What will the world be
like when The Church's accumulated wisdom and knowledge
and experience, its councils of learned, venerable pious men,
are thrust into the kennel by every ignorant laborer or dairy-
maid whom the devil can puff up with the monstrous self-
conceit of being directly inspired from heaven? It will be a
world of blood, of fury, of devastation, of each man striving
for his own hand: in the end a world wrecked back into
barbarism. For now you have only Mahomet and his dupes,
and the Maid and her dupes; but what will it be when every
girl thinks herself a Joan and every man a Mahomet? I shudder
to the very marrow of my bones when I think of it. I have
fought it all my life; and I will fight it to the end. Let all this
woman's sins be forgiven her except only this sin; for it is the
sin against the Holy Ghost; and if she does not recant in the
dust before the world, and submit herself to the last inch of
her soul to her Church, to the fire she shall go if she once falls
into my hand.

WARWICK [*unimpressed*] You feel strongly about it, naturally.

CAUCHON. Do not you?

WARWICK. I am a soldier, not a churchman. As a pilgrim I saw
something of the Mahometans. They were not so illbred as I
had been led to believe. In some respects their conduct compared favorably with ours.

CAUCHON [*displeased*] I have noticed this before. Men go to
the East to convert the infidels. And the infidels pervert them.
The Crusader comes back more than half a Saracen. Not to
mention that all Englishmen are born heretics.

THE CHAPLAIN. Englishmen heretics!!! [*Appealing to Warwick*] My lord: must we endure this? His lordship is beside
himself. How can what an Englishman believes be heresy? It
is a contradiction in terms.

CAUCHON. I absolve you, Messire de Stogumber, on the ground

of invincible ignorance. The thick air of your country does not breed theologians.

WARWICK. You would not say so if you heard us quarrelling about religion, my lord! I am sorry you think I must be either a heretic or a blockhead because, as a travelled man, I know that the followers of Mahomet profess great respect for our Lord, and are more ready to forgive St Peter for being a fisherman than your lordship is to forgive Mahomet for being a camel driver. But at least we can proceed in this matter without bigotry.

CAUCHON. When men call the zeal of the Christian Church bigotry I know what to think.

WARWICK. They are only east and west views of the same thing.

CAUCHON [*bitterly ironical*] O n l y east and west! Only!!

WARWICK. Oh, my Lord Bishop, I am not gainsaying you. You will carry The Church with you; but you have to carry the nobles also. To my mind there is a stronger case against The Maid than the one you have so forcibly put. Frankly, I am not afraid of this girl becoming another Mahomet, and superseding The Church by a great heresy. I think you exaggerate that risk. But have you noticed that in these letters of hers, she proposes to all the kings of Europe, as she has already pressed on Charles, a transaction which would wreck the whole social structure of Christendom?

CAUCHON. Wreck The Church. I tell you so.

WARWICK [*whose patience is wearing out*] My lord: pray get The Church out of your head for a moment; and remember that there are temporal institutions in the world, as well as spiritual ones. I and my peers represent the feudal aristocracy as you represent The Church. We are the temporal power. Well, do you not see how this girl's idea strikes at us?

CAUCHON. How does her idea strike you, except as it strikes at all of us, through The Church?

WARWICK. Her idea is that the kings should give their realms to God, and then reign as God's bailiffs.

CAUCHON [*not interested*] Quite sound theologically, my lord. But the king will hardly care, provided he reign. It is an abstract idea: a mere form of words.

WARWICK. By no means. It is a cunning device to supersede the aristocracy, and make the king sole and absolute autocrat. Instead of the king being merely the first among his peers, he becomes their master. That we cannot suffer: we call no man master. Nominally we hold our lands and dignities from the king, because there must be a keystone to the arch of human society; but we hold our lands in our own hands, and defend them with our own swords and those of our own tenants. Now by The Maid's doctrine the king will take our lands – o u r lands! – and make them a present to God; and God will then vest them wholly in the king.

CAUCHON. Need you fear that? You are the makers of kings after all. York or Lancaster in England, Lancaster or Valois in France: they reign according to your pleasure.

WARWICK. Yes; but only as long as the people follow their feudal lords, and know the king only as a travelling show, owning nothing but the highway that belongs to everybody. If the people's thoughts and hearts were turned to the king, and their lords became only the king's servants in their eyes, the king could break us across his knee one by one; and then what should we be but liveried courtiers in his halls?

CAUCHON. Still you need not fear, my lord. Some men are born kings; and some are born statesmen. The two are seldom the same. Where would the king find counsellors to plan and carry out such a policy for him?

WARWICK [*with a not too friendly smile*] Perhaps in the Church, my lord.

Cauchon, with an equally sour smile, shrugs his shoulders, and does not contradict him.

WARWICK. Strike down the barons; and the cardinals will have it all their own way.

CAUCHON [*conciliatory, dropping his polemical tone*] My lord: we shall not defeat The Maid if we strive against one another. I know well that there is a Will to Power in the world. I know that while it lasts there will be a struggle between the Emperor and the Pope, between the dukes and the political cardinals, between the barons and the kings. The devil divides us and governs. I see you are no friend to The Church: you are an

earl first and last, as I am a churchman first and last. But can
we not sink our differences in the face of a common enemy?
I see now that what is in your mind is not that this girl has
never once mentioned The Church, and thinks only of God
and herself, but that she has never once mentioned the peer-
age, and thinks only of the king and herself.

WARWICK. Quite so. These two ideas of hers are the same idea
at bottom. It goes deep, my lord. It is the protest of the
individual soul against the interference of priest or peer
between the private man and his God. I should call it Protestantism if I had to find a name for it.

CAUCHON [*looking hard at him*] You understand it wonderfully
well, my lord. Scratch an Englishman, and find a Protestant.

WARWICK [*playing the pink of courtesy*] I think you are not
entirely void of sympathy with The Maid's secular heresy, my
lord. I leave you to find a name for it.

CAUCHON. You mistake me, my lord. I have no sympathy with
her political presumptions. But as a priest I have gained a
knowledge of the minds of the common people; and there
you will find yet another most dangerous idea. I can express
it only by such phrases as France for the French, England for
the English, Italy for the Italians, Spain for the Spanish, and
so forth. It is sometimes so narrow and bitter in country folk
that it surprises me that this country girl can rise above the
idea of her village for its villagers. But she can. She does.
When she threatens to drive the English from the soil of
France she is undoubtedly thinking of the whole extent of
country in which French is spoken. To her the French-
speaking people are what the Holy Scriptures describe as a
nation. Call this side of her heresy Nationalism if you will: I
can find you no better name for it. I can only tell you that it is
essentially anti-Catholic and anti-Christian; for the Catholic
Church knows only one realm, and that is the realm of Christ's
kingdom. Divide that kingdom into nations, and you dethrone Christ. Dethrone Christ, and who will stand between
our throats and the sword? The world will perish in a welter
of war.

WARWICK. Well, if you will burn the Protestant, I will burn the

Nationalist, though perhaps I shall not carry Messire John with me there. England for the English will appeal to him.

THE CHAPLAIN. Certainly England for the English goes without saying: it is the simple law of nature. But this woman denies to England her legitimate conquests, given her by God because of her peculiar fitness to rule over less civilized races for their own good. I do not understand what your lordships mean by Protestant and Nationalist: you are too learned and subtle for a poor clerk like myself. But I know as a matter of plain commonsense that the woman is a rebel; and that is enough for me. She rebels against Nature by wearing man's clothes, and fighting. She rebels against The Church by usurping the divine authority of the Pope. She rebels against God by her damnable league with Satan and his evil spirits against our army. And all these rebellions are only excuses for her great rebellion against England. That is not to be endured. Let her perish. Let her burn. Let her not infect the whole flock. It is expedient that one woman die for the people.

WARWICK [rising] My lord: we seem to be agreed.

CAUCHON [rising also, but in protest] I will not imperil my soul. I will uphold the justice of the Church. I will strive to the utmost for this woman's salvation.

WARWICK. I am sorry for the poor girl. I hate these severities. I will spare her if I can.

THE CHAPLAIN [implacably] I would burn her with my own hands.

CAUCHON [blessing him] Sancta simplicitas!

SCENE V

The ambulatory in the cathedral of Rheims, near the door of the vestry. A pillar bears one of the stations of the cross. The organ is playing the people out of the nave after the coronation. Joan is kneeling in prayer before the station. She is beautifully dressed, but still in male attire. The organ ceases as Dunois, also splendidly arrayed, comes into the ambulatory from the vestry.

DUNOIS. Come, Joan! you have had enough praying. After that fit of crying you will catch a chill if you stay here any longer. It is all over: the cathedral is empty; and the streets are full. They are calling for The Maid. We have told them you are staying here alone to pray; but they want to see you again.

JOAN. No: let the king have all the glory.

DUNOIS. He only spoils the show, poor devil. No, Joan: you have crowned him; and you must go through with it.

Joan shakes her head reluctantly.

DUNOIS [*raising her*] Come come! it will be over in a couple of hours. It's better than the bridge at Orleans: eh?

JOAN. Oh, dear Dunois, how I wish it were the bridge at Orleans again! We l i v e d at that bridge.

DUNOIS. Yes, faith, and died too: some of us.

JOAN. Isnt it strange, Jack? I am such a coward: I am frightened beyond words before a battle; but it is so dull afterwards when there is no danger: oh, so dull! dull! dull!

DUNOIS. You must learn to be abstemious in war, just as you are in your food and drink, my little saint.

JOAN. Dear Jack: I think you like me as a soldier likes his comrade.

DUNOIS. You need it, poor innocent child of God. You have not many friends at court.

JOAN. Why do all these courtiers and knights and churchmen hate me? What have I done to them? I have asked nothing for myself except that my village shall not be taxed; for we cannot afford war taxes. I have brought them luck and victory; I have set them right when they were doing all sorts of stupid things:

I have crowned Charles and made him a real king; and all the honors he is handing out have gone to them. Then why do they not love me?

DUNOIS [*rallying her*] Sim-ple-ton! Do you expect stupid people to love you for shewing them up? Do blundering old military dug-outs love the successful young captains who supersede them? Do ambitious politicians love the climbers who take the front seats from them? Do archbishops enjoy being played off their own altars, even by saints? Why, I should be jealous of you myself if I were ambitious enough.

JOAN. You are the pick of the basket here, Jack: the only friend I have among all these nobles. I'll wager your mother was from the country. I will go back to the farm when I have taken Paris.

DUNOIS. I am not so sure that they will let you take Paris.

JOAN [*startled*] What!

DUNOIS. I should have taken it myself before this if they had all been sound about it. Some of them would rather Paris took you, I think. So take care.

JOAN. Jack: the world is too wicked for me. If the goddams and the Burgundians do not make an end of me, the French will. Only for my voices I should lose all heart. That is why I had to steal away to pray here alone after the coronation. I'll tell you something, Jack. It is in the bells I hear my voices. Not today, when they all rang: that was nothing but jangling. But here in this corner, where the bells come down from heaven, and the echoes linger, or in the fields, where they come from a distance through the quiet of the countryside, my voices are in them. [*The cathedral clock chimes the quarter*] Hark! [*She becomes rapt*] Do you hear? 'Dear-child-of-God': just what you said. At the half-hour they will say 'Be-brave-go-on.' At the three-quarters they will say 'I-am-thy-Help.' But it is at the hour, when the great bell goes after 'God-will-save-France': it is then that St Margaret and St Catherine and sometimes even the blessed Michael will say things that I cannot tell beforehand. Then, oh then –

DUNOIS [*interrupting her kindly but not sympathetically*] Then, Joan, we shall hear whatever we fancy in the booming of the bell. You make me uneasy when you talk about your voices:

I should think you were a bit cracked if I hadnt noticed that you give me very sensible reasons for what you do, though I hear you telling others you are only obeying Madame Saint Catherine.

JOAN [*crossly*] Well, I have to find reasons for you, because you do not believe in my voices. But the voices come first; and I find the reasons after: whatever you may choose to believe.

DUNOIS. Are you angry, Joan?

JOAN. Yes. [*Smiling*] No: not with you. I wish you were one of the village babies.

DUNOIS. Why?

JOAN. I could nurse you for awhile.

DUNOIS. You are a bit of a woman after all.

JOAN. No: not a bit: I am a soldier and nothing else. Soldiers always nurse children when they get a chance.

DUNOIS. That is true. [*He laughs*].

   King Charles, with Bluebeard on his left and La Hire on his right, comes from the vestry, where he has been disrobing. Joan shrinks away behind the pillar. Dunois is left between Charles and La Hire.

DUNOIS. Well, your Majesty is an anointed king at last. How do you like it?

CHARLES. I would not go through it again to be emperor of the sun and moon. The weight of those robes! I thought I should have dropped when they loaded that crown on to me. And the famous holy oil they talked so much about was rancid: phew! The Archbishop must be nearly dead: his robes must have weighed a ton: they are stripping him still in the vestry.

DUNOIS [*drily*] Your majesty should wear armor oftener. That would accustom you to heavy dressing.

CHARLES. Yes: the old jibe! Well, I am not going to wear armor: fighting is not my job. Where is The Maid?

JOAN [*coming forward between Charles and Bluebeard, and falling on her knee*] Sire: I have made you king: my work is done. I am going back to my father's farm.

CHARLES [*surprised, but relieved*] Oh, are you? Well, that will be very nice.

   Joan rises, deeply discouraged.

CHARLES [*continuing heedlessly*] A healthy life, you know.

DUNOIS. But a dull one.

BLUEBEARD. You will find the petticoats tripping you up after leaving them off for so long.

LA HIRE. You will miss the fighting. It's a bad habit, but a grand one, and the hardest of all to break yourself of.

CHARLES [*anxiously*] Still, we dont want you to stay if you would really rather go home.

JOAN [*bitterly*] I know well that none of you will be sorry to see me go. [*She turns her shoulder to Charles and walks past him to the more congenial neighborhood of Dunois and La Hire*].

LA HIRE. Well, I shall be able to swear when I want to. But I shall miss you at times.

JOAN. La Hire: in spite of all your sins and swears we shall meet in heaven; for I love you as I love Pitou, my old sheep dog. Pitou could kill a wolf. You will kill the English wolves until they go back to their country and become good dogs of God, will you not?

LA HIRE. You and I together: yes.

JOAN. No: I shall last only a year from the beginning.

ALL THE OTHERS. What!

JOAN. I know it somehow.

DUNOIS. Nonsense!

JOAN. Jack: do you think you will be able to drive them out?

DUNOIS [*with quiet conviction*] Yes: I shall drive them out. They beat us because we thought battles were tournaments and ransom markets. We played the fool while the goddams took war seriously. But I have learnt my lesson, and taken their measure. They have no roots here. I have beaten them before; and I shall beat them again.

JOAN. You will not be cruel to them, Jack?

DUNOIS. The goddams will not yield to tender handling. We did not begin it.

JOAN [*suddenly*] Jack: before I go home, let us take Paris.

CHARLES [*terrified*] Oh no no. We shall lose everything we have gained. Oh dont let us have any more fighting. We can make a very good treaty with the Duke of Burgundy.

JOAN. Treaty! [*She stamps with impatience*].

CHARLES. Well, why not, now that I am crowned and anointed? Oh, that oil!

> *The Archbishop comes from the vestry, and joins the group between Charles and Bluebeard.*

CHARLES. Archbishop: The Maid wants to start fighting again.

THE ARCHBISHOP. Have we ceased fighting, then? Are we at peace?

CHARLES. No: I suppose not; but let us be content with what we have done. Let us make a treaty. Our luck is too good to last; and now is our chance to stop before it turns.

JOAN. Luck! God has fought for us; and you call it luck! And you would stop while there are still Englishmen on this holy earth of dear France!

THE ARCHBISHOP [*sternly*] Maid: the king addressed himself to me, not to you. You forget yourself. You very often forget yourself.

JOAN [*unabashed, and rather roughly*] Then speak, you; and tell him that it is not God's will that he should take his hand from the plough.

THE ARCHBISHOP. If I am not so glib with the name of God as you are, it is because I interpret His will with the authority of the Church and of my sacred office. When you first came you respected it, and would not have dared to speak as you are now speaking. You came clothed with the virtue of humility; and because God blessed your enterprises accordingly, you have stained yourself with the sin of pride. The old Greek tragedy is rising among us. It is the chastisement of hubris.

CHARLES. Yes: she thinks she knows better than everyone else.

JOAN [*distressed, but naïvely incapable of seeing the effect she is producing*] But I d o know better than any of you seem to. And I am not proud: I never speak unless I know I am right.

BLUEBEARD
CHARLES } [*exclaiming together*] { Ha ha!
Just so.

THE ARCHBISHOP. How do you know you are right?

JOAN. I always know. My voices –

CHARLES. Oh, your voices, your voices. Why dont the voices come to me? I am king, not you.

JOAN. They do come to you; but you do not hear them. You
have not sat in the field in the evening listening for them.
When the angelus rings you cross yourself and have done
with it; but if you prayed from your heart, and listened to the
thrilling of the bells in the air after they stop ringing, you
would hear the voices as well as I do. [*Turning brusquely
from him*] But what voices do you need to tell you what the
blacksmith can tell you: that you must strike while the iron is
hot? I tell you we must make a dash at Compiègne and relieve
it as we relieved Orleans. Then Paris will open its gates; or if
not, we will break through them. What is your crown worth
without your capital?

LA HIRE. That is what I say too. We shall go through them like
a red hot shot through a pound of butter. What do you say,
Bastard?

DUNOIS. If our cannon balls were all as hot as your head, and
we had enough of them, we should conquer the earth, no
doubt. Pluck and impetuosity are good servants in war, but
bad masters: they have delivered us into the hands of the
English every time we have trusted to them. We never know
when we are beaten: that is our great fault.

JOAN. You never know when you are victorious: that is a worse
fault. I shall have to make you carry looking-glasses in battle
to convince you that the English have not cut off all your
noses. You would have been besieged in Orleans still, you
and your councils of war, if I had not made you attack. You
should always attack; and if you only hold on long enough
the enemy will stop first. You dont know how to begin a
battle; and you dont know how to use your cannons. And
I do.

  She squats down on the flags with crossed ankles, pouting.

DUNOIS. I know what you think of us, General Joan.

JOAN. Never mind that, Jack. Tell them what you think of me.

DUNOIS. I think that God was on your side; for I have not
forgotten how the wind changed, and how our hearts changed
when you came; and by my faith I shall never deny that it was
in your sign that we conquered. But I tell you as a soldier that
God is no man's daily drudge, and no maid's either. If you

are worthy of it He will sometimes snatch you out of the jaws
of death and set you on your feet again; but that is all: once
on your feet you must fight with all your might and all your
craft. For He has to be fair to your enemy too: dont forget
that. Well, He set us on our feet through you at Orleans; and
the glory of it has carried us through a few good battles here
to the coronation. But if we presume on it further, and trust
to God to do the work we should do ourselves, we shall be
defeated; and serve us right!

JOAN. But –

DUNOIS. Sh! I have not finished. Do not think, any of you, that
these victories of ours were won without generalship. King
Charles: you have said no word in your proclamations of my
part in this campaign; and I make no complaint of that; for
the people will run after The Maid and her miracles and not
after the Bastard's hard work finding troops for her and
feeding them. But I know exactly how much God did for us
through The Maid, and how much He left me to do by my
own wits; and I tell you that your little hour of miracles is
over, and that from this time on he who plays the war game
best will win – if the luck is on his side.

JOAN. Ah! if, if, if, if! If ifs and ans were pots and pans there'd
be no need of tinkers. [*Rising impetuously*] I tell y o u, Bastard, your art of war is no use, because your knights are no
good for real fighting. War is only a game to them, like tennis
and all their other games: they make rules as to what is fair
and what is not fair, and heap armor on themselves and on
their poor horses to keep out the arrows; and when they fall
they cant get up, and have to wait for their squires to come
and lift them to arrange about the ransom with the man that
has poked them off their horse. Cant you see that all the like
of that is gone by and done with? What use is armor against
gunpowder? And if it was, do you think men that are fighting
for France and for God will stop to bargain about ransoms,
as half your knights live by doing? No: they will fight to win;
and they will give up their lives out of their own hand into
the hand of God when they go into battle, as I do. Common
folks understand this. They cannot afford armor and cannot

pay ransoms; but they followed me half naked into the moat and up the ladder and over the wall. With them it is my life or thine, and God defend the right! You may shake your head, Jack; and Bluebeard may twirl his billygoat's beard and cock his nose at me; but remember the day your knights and captains refused to follow me to attack the English at Orleans! You locked the gates to keep me in; and it was the townsfolk and the common people that followed me, and forced the gate, and shewed you the way to fight in earnest.

BLUEBEARD [offended] Not content with being Pope Joan, you must be Caesar and Alexander as well.

THE ARCHBISHOP. Pride will have a fall, Joan.

JOAN. Oh, never mind whether it is pride or not: is it true? is it commonsense?

LA HIRE. It is true. Half of us are afraid of having our handsome noses broken; and the other half are out for paying off their mortgages. Let her have her way, Dunois: she does not know everything; but she has got hold of the right end of the stick. Fighting is not what it was; and those who know least about it often make the best job of it.

DUNOIS. I know all that. I do not fight in the old way: I have learnt the lesson of Agincourt, of Poitiers and Crecy. I know how many lives any move of mine will cost; and if the move is worth the cost I make it and pay the cost. But Joan never counts the cost at all: she goes ahead and trusts to God: she thinks she has God in her pocket. Up to now she has had the numbers on her side; and she has won. But I know Joan; and I see that some day she will go ahead when she has only ten men to do the work of a hundred. And then she will find that God is on the side of the big battalions. She will be taken by the enemy. And the lucky man that makes the capture will receive sixteen thousand pounds from the Earl of Ouareek.

JOAN [flattered] Sixteen thousand pounds! Eh, laddie, have they offered that for me? There cannot be so much money in the world.

DUNOIS. There is, in England. And now tell me, all of you, which of you will lift a finger to save Joan once the English have got her? I speak first, for the army. The day after she has been dragged from her horse by a goddam or a Burgundian, and he is not struck dead: the day after she is locked in a dungeon, and the bars and bolts do not fly open at the touch of St Peter's angel: the day when the enemy finds out that she is as vulnerable as I am and not a bit more invincible, she will not be worth the life of a single soldier to us; and I will not risk that life, much as I cherish her as a companion-in-arms.

JOAN. I dont blame you, Jack: you are right. I am not worth one soldier's life if God lets me be beaten; but France may think me worth my ransom after what God has done for her through me.

CHARLES. I tell you I have no money; and this coronation, which is all your fault, has cost me the last farthing I can borrow.

JOAN. The Church is richer than you. I put my trust in the Church.

THE ARCHBISHOP. Woman: they will drag you through the streets, and burn you as a witch.

JOAN [running to him] Oh, my lord, do not say that. It is impossible. I a witch!

THE ARCHBISHOP. Peter Cauchon knows his business. The University of Paris has burnt a woman for saying that what you have done was well done, and according to God.

JOAN [bewildered] But why? What sense is there in it? What I have done is according to God. They could not burn a woman for speaking the truth.

THE ARCHBISHOP. They did.

JOAN. But you know that she was speaking the truth. You would not let them burn me.

THE ARCHBISHOP. How could I prevent them?

JOAN. You would speak in the name of the Church. You are a great prince of the Church. I would go anywhere with your blessing to protect me.

THE ARCHBISHOP. I have no blessing for you while you are proud and disobedient.

JOAN. Oh, why will you go on saying things like that? I am not proud and disobedient. I am a poor girl, and so ignorant that I do not know A from B. How could I be proud? And how

can you say that I am disobedient when I always obey my
voices, because they come from God.

THE ARCHBISHOP. The voice of God on earth is the voice of
the Church Militant; and all the voices that come to you are
the echoes of your own wilfulness.

JOAN. It is not true.

THE ARCHBISHOP [*flushing angrily*] You tell the Archbishop
in his cathedral that he lies; and yet you say you are not proud
and disobedient.

JOAN. I never said you lied. It was you that as good as said my
voices lied. When have they ever lied? If you will not believe
in them: even if they are only the echoes of my own commonsense, are they not always right? and are not your earthly
counsels always wrong?

THE ARCHBISHOP [*indignantly*] It is waste of time admonishing you.

CHARLES. It always comes back to the same thing. She is right;
and everyone else is wrong.

THE ARCHBISHOP. Take this as your last warning. If you perish
through setting your private judgment above the instructions
of your spiritual directors, the Church disowns you, and
leaves you to whatever fate your presumption may bring
upon you. The Bastard has told you that if you persist in
setting up your military conceit above the counsels of your
commanders –

DUNOIS [*interposing*] To put it quite exactly, if you attempt to
relieve the garrison in Compiègne without the same superiority in numbers you had at Orleans –

THE ARCHBISHOP. The army will disown you, and will not
rescue you. And His Majesty the King has told you that the
throne has not the means of ransoming you.

CHARLES. Not a penny.

THE ARCHBISHOP. You stand alone: absolutely alone, trusting
to your own conceit, your own ignorance, your own head-
strong presumption, your own impiety in hiding all these sins
under the cloak of a trust in God. When you pass through
these doors into the sunlight, the crowd will cheer you. They
will bring you their little children and their invalids to heal:

they will kiss your hands and feet, and do what they can, poor simple souls, to turn your head, and madden you with the self-confidence that is leading you to your destruction. But you will be none the less alone: they cannot save you. We and we only can stand between you and the stake at which our enemies have burnt that wretched woman in Paris.

JOAN [*her eyes skyward*] I have better friends and better counsel than yours.

THE ARCHBISHOP. I see that I am speaking in vain to a hardened heart. You reject our protection, and are determined to turn us all against you. In future, then, fend for yourself; and if you fail, God have mercy on your soul.

DUNOIS. That is the truth, Joan. Heed it.

JOAN. Where would you all have been now if I had heeded that sort of truth? There is no help, no counsel, in any of you. Yes: I a m alone on earth: I have always been alone. My father told my brothers to drown me if I would not stay to mind his sheep while France was bleeding to death: France might perish if only our lambs were safe. I thought France would have friends at the court of the king of France; and I find only wolves fighting for pieces of her poor torn body. I thought God would have friends everywhere, because He is the friend of everyone; and in my innocence I believed that you who now cast me out would be like strong towers to keep harm from me. But I am wiser now; and nobody is any the worse for being wiser. Do not think you can frighten me by telling me that I am alone. France is alone; and God is alone; and what is my loneliness before the loneliness of my country and my God? I see now that the loneliness of God is His strength: what would He be if He listened to your jealous little counsels? Well, my loneliness shall be my strength too; it is better to be alone with God: His friendship will not fail me, nor His counsel, nor His love. In His strength I will dare, and dare, and dare, until I die. I will go out now to the common people, and let the love in their eyes comfort me for the hate in yours. You will all be glad to see me burnt; but if I go through the fire I shall go through it to their hearts for ever and ever. And so, God be with me!

*She goes from them. They stare after her in glum silence
for a moment. Then Gilles de Rais twirls his beard.*

BLUEBEARD. You know, the woman is quite impossible. I
dont dislike her, really; but what are you to do with such a
character?

DUNOIS. As God is my judge, if she fell into the Loire I would
jump in in full armor to fish her out. But if she plays the fool
at Compiègne, and gets caught, I must leave her to her doom.

LA HIRE. Then you had better chain me up; for I could follow
her to hell when the spirit rises in her like that.

THE ARCHBISHOP. She disturbs my judgment too: there is a
dangerous power in her outbursts. But the pit is open at her
feet; and for good or evil we cannot turn her from it.

CHARLES. If only she would keep quiet, or go home!

They follow her dispiritedly.

SCENE VI

Rouen, 30th May 1431. A great stone hall in the castle, arranged for a trial-at-law, but not a trial-by-jury, the court being the Bishop's court with the Inquisition participating: hence there are two raised chairs side by side for the Bishop and the Inquisitor as judges. Rows of chairs radiating from them at an obtuse angle are for the canons, the doctors of law and theology, and the Dominican monks, who act as assessors. In the angle is a table for the scribes, with stools. There is also a heavy rough wooden stool for the prisoner. All these are at the inner end of the hall. The further end is open to the courtyard through a row of arches. The court is shielded from the weather by screens and curtains.

Looking down the great hall from the middle of the inner end, the judicial chairs and scribes' table are to the right. The prisoner's stool is to the left. There are arched doors right and left. It is a fine sunshiny May morning.

Warwick comes in through the arched doorway on the judges' side, followed by his page.

THE PAGE [*pertly*] I suppose your lordship is aware that we have no business here. This is an ecclesiastical court; and we are only the secular arm.

WARWICK. I am aware of that fact. Will it please your impudence to find the Bishop of Beauvais for me, and give him a hint that he can have a word with me here before the trial, if he wishes?

THE PAGE [*going*] Yes, my lord.

WARWICK. And mind you behave yourself. Do not address him as Pious Peter.

THE PAGE. No, my lord. I shall be kind to him, because, when The Maid is brought in, Pious Peter will have to pick a peck of pickled pepper.

Cauchon enters through the same door with a Dominican monk and a canon, the latter carrying a brief.

THE PAGE. The Right Reverend his lordship the Bishop of Beauvais. And two other reverend gentlemen.

WARWICK. Get out; and see that we are not interrupted.

THE PAGE. Right, my lord [*he vanishes airily*].

CAUCHON. I wish your lordship good-morrow.

WARWICK. Good-morrow to your lordship. Have I had the pleasure of meeting your friends before? I think not.

CAUCHON [*introducing the monk, who is on his right*] This, my lord, is Brother John Lemaître, of the order of St Dominic. He is acting as deputy for the Chief Inquisitor into the evil of heresy in France. Brother John: the Earl of Warwick.

WARWICK. Your Reverence is most welcome. We have no Inquisitor in England, unfortunately; though we miss him greatly, especially on occasions like the present.

The Inquisitor smiles patiently, and bows. He is a mild elderly gentleman, but has evident reserves of authority and firmness.

CAUCHON [*introducing the Canon, who is on his left*] This gentleman is Canon John D'Estivet, of the Chapter of Bayeux. He is acting as Promoter.

WARWICK. Promoter?

CAUCHON. Prosecutor, you would call him in civil law.

WARWICK. Ah! prosecutor. Quite, quite. I am very glad to make your acquaintance, Canon D'Estivet.

D'Estivet bows. [He is on the young side of middle age, well mannered, but vulpine beneath his veneer].

WARWICK. May I ask what stage the proceedings have reached? It is now more than nine months since The Maid was captured at Compiègne by the Burgundians. It is fully four months since I bought her from the Burgundians for a very handsome sum, solely that she might be brought to justice. It is very nearly three months since I delivered her up to you, my Lord Bishop, as a person suspected of heresy. May I suggest that you are taking a rather unconscionable time to make up your minds about a very plain case? Is this trial never going to end?

THE INQUISITOR [*smiling*] It has not yet begun, my lord.

WARWICK. Not yet begun! Why, you have been at it eleven weeks!

CAUCHON. We have not been idle, my lord. We have held fifteen examinations of The Maid: six public and nine private.

THE INQUISITOR [*always patiently smiling*] You see, my lord, I have been present at only two of these examinations. They were proceedings of the Bishop's court solely, and not of the Holy Office. I have only just decided to associate myself – that is, to associate the Holy Inquisition – with the Bishop's court. I did not at first think that this was a case of heresy at all. I regarded it as a political case, and The Maid as a prisoner of war. But having now been present at two of the examinations, I must admit that this seems to be one of the gravest cases of heresy within my experience. Therefore everything is now in order, and we proceed to trial this morning. [*He moves towards the judicial chairs*].

CAUCHON. This moment, if your lordship's convenience allows.

WARWICK [*graciously*] Well, that is good news, gentlemen. I will not attempt to conceal from you that our patience was becoming strained.

CAUCHON. So I gathered from the threats of your soldiers to drown those of our people who favor The Maid.

WARWICK. Dear me! At all events their intentions were friendly to y o u, my lord.

CAUCHON [*sternly*] I hope not. I am determined that the woman shall have a fair hearing. The justice of the Church is not a mockery, my lord.

THE INQUISITOR [*returning*] Never has there been a fairer examination within my experience, my lord. The Maid needs no lawyers to take her part: she will be tried by her most faithful friends, all ardently desirous to save her soul from perdition.

D'ESTIVET. Sir: I am the Promoter; and it has been my painful duty to present the case against the girl; but believe me, I would throw up my case today and hasten to her defence if I did not know that men far my superiors in learning and piety, in eloquence and persuasiveness, have been sent to reason with her, to explain to her the danger she is running, and the ease with which she may avoid it. [*Suddenly bursting into forensic eloquence, to the disgust of Cauchon and the Inquisitor, who have listened to him so far with patronizing approval*] Men have dared to say that we are acting from

hate; but God is our witness that they lie. Have we tortured
her? No. Have we ceased to exhort her; to implore her to
have pity on herself; to come to the bosom of her Church as
an erring but beloved child? Have we –

CAUCHON [*interrupting drily*] Take care, Canon. All that you
say is true; but if you make his lordship believe it I will not
answer for your life, and hardly for my own.

WARWICK [*deprecating, but by no means denying*] Oh, my lord,
you are very hard on us poor English. But we certainly do not
share your pious desire to save The Maid: in fact I tell you
now plainly that her death is a political necessity which I
regret but cannot help. If the Church lets her go –

CAUCHON [*with fierce and menacing pride*] If the Church lets
her go, woe to the man, were he the Emperor himself, who
dares lay a finger on her! The Church is not subject to political
necessity, my lord.

THE INQUISITOR [*interposing smoothly*] You need have no
anxiety about the result, my lord. You have an invincible ally
in the matter: one who is far more determined than you that
she shall burn.

WARWICK. And who is this very convenient partisan, may I
ask?

THE INQUISITOR. The Maid herself. Unless you put a gag in
her mouth you cannot prevent her from convicting herself ten
times over every time she opens it.

D'ESTIVET. That is perfectly true, my lord. My hair bristles
on my head when I hear so young a creature utter such
blasphemies.

WARWICK. Well, by all means do your best for her if you are quite
sure it will be of no avail. [*Looking hard at Cauchon*] I should
be sorry to have to act without the blessing of the Church.

CAUCHON [*with a mixture of cynical admiration and contempt*]
And yet they say Englishmen are hypocrites! You play for
your side, my lord, even at the peril of your soul. I cannot but
admire such devotion; but I dare not go so far myself. I fear
damnation.

WARWICK. If we feared anything we could never govern England, my lord. Shall I send your people in to you?

CAUCHON. Yes: it will be very good of your lordship to withdraw and allow the court to assemble.

*Warwick turns on his heel, and goes out through the court-
yard. Cauchon takes one of the judicial seats; and D'Estivet
sits at the scribes' table, studying his brief.*

CAUCHON [*casually, as he makes himself comfortable*] What
scoundrels these English nobles are!

THE INQUISITOR [*taking the other judicial chair on Cauchon's
left*] All secular power makes men scoundrels. They are
not trained for the work; and they have not the Apostolic
Succession. Our own nobles are just as bad.

*The Bishop's assessors hurry into the hall, headed by
Chaplain de Stogumber and Canon de Courcelles, a young
priest of 30. The scribes sit at the table, leaving a chair
vacant opposite D'Estivet. Some of the assessors take their
seats: others stand chatting, waiting for the proceedings to
begin formally. De Stogumber, aggrieved and obstinate, will
not take his seat: neither will the Canon, who stands on
his right.*

CAUCHON. Good morning, Master de Stogumber. [*To the
Inquisitor*] Chaplain to the Cardinal of England.

THE CHAPLAIN [*correcting him*] Of Winchester, my lord. I
have to make a protest, my lord.

CAUCHON. You make a great many.

THE CHAPLAIN. I am not without support, my lord. Here is
Master de Courcelles, Canon of Paris, who associates himself
with me in my protest.

CAUCHON. Well, what is the matter?

THE CHAPLAIN [*sulkily*] Speak you, Master de Courcelles,
since I do not seem to enjoy his lordship's confidence. [*He sits
down in dudgeon next to Cauchon, on his right*].

COURCELLES. My lord: we have been at great pains to draw
up an indictment of The Maid on sixty-four counts. We are
now told that they have been reduced, without consulting us.

THE INQUISITOR. Master de Courcelles: I am the culprit. I am
overwhelmed with admiration for the zeal displayed in your
sixty-four counts; but in accusing a heretic, as in other things,
enough is enough. Also you must remember that all the

members of the court are not so subtle and profound as you, and that some of your very great learning might appear to them to be very great nonsense. Therefore I have thought it well to have your sixty-four articles cut down to twelve –

COURCELLES [*thunderstruck*] Twelve!!!

THE INQUISITOR. Twelve will, believe me, be quite enough for your purpose.

THE CHAPLAIN. But some of the most important points have been reduced almost to nothing. For instance, The Maid has actually declared that the blessed saints Margaret and Catherine, and the holy Archangel Michael, spoke to her in French. That is a vital point.

THE INQUISITOR. You think, doubtless, that they should have spoken in Latin?

CAUCHON. No: he thinks they should have spoken in English.

THE CHAPLAIN. Naturally, my lord.

THE INQUISITOR. Well, as we are all here agreed, I think, that these voices of The Maid are the voices of evil spirits tempting her to her damnation, it would not be very courteous to you, Master de Stogumber, or to the King of England, to assume that English is the devil's native language. So let it pass. The matter is not wholly omitted from the twelve articles. Pray take your places, gentlemen; and let us proceed to business.

All who have not taken their seats, do so.

THE CHAPLAIN. Well, I protest. That is all.

COURCELLES. I think it hard that all our work should go for nothing. It is only another example of the diabolical influence which this woman exercises over the court. [*He takes his chair, which is on the Chaplain's right*].

CAUCHON. Do you suggest that I am under diabolical influence?

COURCELLES. I suggest nothing, my lord. But it seems to me that there is a conspiracy here to hush up the fact that The Maid stole the Bishop of Senlis's horse.

CAUCHON [*keeping his temper with difficulty*] This is not a police court. Are we to waste our time on such rubbish?

COURCELLES [*rising, shocked*] My lord: do you call the Bishop's horse rubbish?

THE INQUISITOR [*blandly*] Master de Courcelles: The Maid alleges that she paid handsomely for the Bishop's horse, and that if he did not get the money the fault was not hers. As that may be true, the point is one on which The Maid may well be acquitted.

COURCELLES. Yes, if it were an ordinary horse. But the Bishop's horse! how can she be acquitted for that? [*He sits down again, bewildered and discouraged*].

THE INQUISITOR. I submit to you, with great respect, that if we persist in trying The Maid on trumpery issues on which we may have to declare her innocent, she may escape us on the great main issue of heresy, on which she seems so far to insist on her own guilt. I will ask you, therefore, to say nothing, when The Maid is brought before us, of these stealings of horses, and dancings round fairy trees with the village children, and prayings at haunted wells, and a dozen other things which you were diligently inquiring into until my arrival. There is not a village girl in France against whom you could not prove such things: they all dance round haunted trees, and pray at magic wells. Some of them would steal the Pope's horse if they got the chance. Heresy, gentlemen, heresy is the charge we have to try. The detection and suppression of heresy is my peculiar business: I am here as an inquisitor, not as an ordinary magistrate. Stick to the heresy, gentlemen; and leave the other matters alone.

CAUCHON. I may say that we have sent to the girl's village to make inquiries about her, and there is practically nothing serious against her.

THE CHAPLAIN   [*rising and*   Nothing serious, my lord –
COURCELLES   *clamoring*   What! The fairy tree not –
                  together]

CAUCHON [*out of patience*] Be silent, gentlemen; or speak one at a time.

   Courcelles collapses into his chair, intimidated.

THE CHAPLAIN [*sulkily resuming his seat*] That is what The Maid said to us last Friday.

CAUCHON. I wish you had followed her counsel, sir. When I say nothing serious, I mean nothing that men of sufficiently

large mind to conduct an inquiry like this would consider
serious. I agree with my colleague the Inquisitor that it is on
the count of heresy that we must proceed.

LADVENU [*a young but ascetically fine-drawn Dominican who
is sitting next Courcelles, on his right*] But is there any great
harm in the girl's heresy? Is it not merely her simplicity? Many
saints have said as much as Joan.

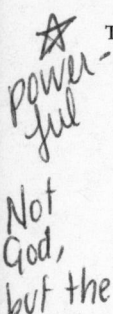

THE INQUISITOR [*dropping his blandness and speaking very
gravely*] Brother Martin: if you had seen what I have seen of
heresy, you would not think it a light thing even in its most
apparently harmless and even lovable and pious origins.
Heresy begins with people who are to all appearance better
than their neighbors. A gentle and pious girl, or a young man
who has obeyed the command of our Lord by giving all his
riches to the poor, and putting on the garb of poverty, the life
of austerity, and the rule of humility and charity, may be the
founder of a heresy that will wreck both Church and Empire
if not ruthlessly stamped out in time. The records of the holy
Inquisition are full of histories we dare not give to the world,
because they are beyond the belief of honest men and innocent
women; yet they all began with saintly simpletons. I have seen
this again and again. Mark what I say: the woman who
quarrels with her clothes, and puts on the dress of a man, is
like the man who throws off his fur gown and dresses like
<u>John the Baptist</u>: they are followed, as surely as the night
follows the day, by bands of wild women and men who refuse
to wear any clothes at all. When maids will neither marry nor
take regular vows, and men reject marriage and exalt their
lusts into divine inspirations, then, as surely as the summer
follows the spring, they begin with polygamy, and end by
incest. Heresy at first seems innocent and even laudable; but
it ends in such a monstrous horror of unnatural wickedness
that the most tender-hearted among you, if you saw it at work
as I have seen it, would clamor against the mercy of the
Church in dealing with it. For two hundred years the Holy
Office has striven with these diabolical madnesses; and it
knows that they begin always by vain and ignorant persons
setting up their own judgment against the Church, and taking

it upon themselves to be the interpreters of God's will. You must not fall into the common error of mistaking these simpletons for liars and hypocrites. They believe honestly and sincerely that their diabolical inspiration is divine. Therefore you must be on your guard against your natural compassion. You are all, I hope, merciful men: how else could you have devoted your lives to the service of our gentle Savior? You are going to see before you a young girl, pious and chaste; for I must tell you, gentlemen, that the things said of her by our English friends are supported by no evidence, whilst there is abundant testimony that her excesses have been excesses of religion and charity and not of worldliness and wantonness. This girl is not one of those whose hard features are the sign of hard hearts, and whose brazen looks and lewd demeanor condemn them before they are accused. The devilish pride that has led her into her present peril has left no mark on her countenance. Strange as it may seem to you, it has even left no mark on her character outside those special matters in which she is proud; so that you will see a diabolical pride and a natural humility seated side by side in the selfsame soul. Therefore be on your guard. God forbid that I should tell you to harden your hearts; for her punishment if we condemn her will be so cruel that we should forfeit our own hope of divine mercy were there one grain of malice against her in our hearts. But if you hate cruelty – and if any man here does not hate it I command him on his soul's salvation to quit this holy court – I say, if you hate cruelty, remember that nothing is so cruel in its consequences as the toleration of heresy. Remember also that no court of law can be so cruel as the common people are to those whom they suspect of heresy. The heretic in the hands of the Holy Office is safe from violence, is assured of a fair trial, and cannot suffer death, even when guilty, if repentance follows sin. Innumerable lives of heretics have been saved because the Holy Office has taken them out of the hands of the people, and because the people have yielded them up, knowing that the Holy Office would deal with them. Before the Holy Inquisition existed, and even now when its officers are not within reach, the unfortunate wretch suspected of heresy, perhaps quite ignorantly and unjustly, is stoned, torn in pieces, drowned, burned in his house with all his innocent children, without a trial, unshriven, unburied save as a dog is buried: all of them deeds hateful to God and most cruel to man. Gentlemen: I am compassionate by nature as well as by my profession; and though the work I have to do may seem cruel to those who do not know how much more cruel it would be to leave it undone, I would go to the stake myself sooner than do it if I did not know its righteousness, its necessity, its essential mercy. I ask you to address yourself to this trial in that conviction. Anger is a bad counsellor: cast out anger. Pity is sometimes worse: cast out pity. But do not cast out mercy. Remember only that justice comes first. Have you anything to say, my lord, before we proceed to trial?

CAUCHON. You have spoken for me, and spoken better than I could. I do not see how any sane man could disagree with a word that has fallen from you. But this I will add. The crude heresies of which you have told us are horrible; but their horror is like that of the black death: they rage for a while and then die out, because sound and sensible men will not under any incitement be reconciled to nakedness and incest and polygamy and the like. But we are confronted today throughout Europe with a heresy that is spreading among men not weak in mind nor diseased in brain: nay, the stronger the mind, the more obstinate the heretic. It is neither discredited by fantastic extremes nor corrupted by the common lusts of the flesh; but it, too, sets up the private judgment of the single erring mortal against the considered wisdom and experience of the Church. The mighty structure of Catholic Christendom will never be shaken by naked madmen or by the sins of Moab and Ammon. But it may be betrayed from within, and brought to barbarous ruin and desolation, by this arch heresy which the English Commander calls Protestantism.

THE ASSESSORS [whispering] Protestantism! What was that? What does the Bishop mean? Is it a new heresy? The English Commander, he said. Did y o u ever hear of Protestantism? etc., etc.

CAUCHON [*continuing*] And that reminds me. What provision has the Earl of Warwick made for the defence of the secular arm should The Maid prove obdurate, and the people be moved to pity her?

THE CHAPLAIN. Have no fear on that score, my lord. The noble earl has eight hundred men-at-arms at the gates. She will not slip through our English fingers even if the whole city be on her side.

CAUCHON [*revolted*] Will you not add, God grant that she repent and purge her sin?

THE CHAPLAIN. That does not seem to me to be consistent; but of course I agree with your lordship.

CAUCHON [*giving him up with a shrug of contempt*] The court sits.

THE INQUISITOR. Let the accused be brought in.

LADVENU [*calling*] The accused. Let her be brought in.

Joan, chained by the ankles, is brought in through the arched door behind the prisoner's stool by a guard of English soldiers. With them is the Executioner and his assistants. They lead her to the prisoner's stool, and place themselves behind it after taking off her chain. She wears a page's black suit. Her long imprisonment and the strain of the examinations which have preceded the trial have left their mark on her; but her vitality still holds: she confronts the court unabashed, without a trace of the awe which their formal solemnity seems to require for the complete success of its impressiveness.

THE INQUISITOR [*kindly*] Sit down, Joan. [*She sits on the prisoner's stool*]. You look very pale today. Are you not well?

JOAN. Thank you kindly: I am well enough. But the Bishop sent me some carp; and it made me ill.

CAUCHON. I am sorry. I told them to see that it was fresh.

JOAN. You meant to be good to me, I know; but it is a fish that does not agree with me. The English thought you were trying to poison me –

CAUCHON
THE CHAPLAIN } [*together*] { What!
No, my lord.

JOAN [*continuing*] They are determined that I shall be burnt as a witch; and they sent their doctor to cure me; but he was forbidden to bleed me because the silly people believe that a witch's witchery leaves her if she is bled; so he only called me filthy names. Why do you leave me in the hands of the English? I should be in the hands of the Church. And why must I be chained by the feet to a log of wood? Are you afraid I will fly away?

D'ESTIVET [harshly] Woman: it is not for you to question the court: it is for us to question you.

COURCELLES. When you were left unchained, did you not try to escape by jumping from a tower sixty feet high? If you cannot fly like a witch, how is it that you are still alive?

JOAN. I suppose because the tower was not so high then. It has grown higher every day since you began asking me questions about it.

D'ESTIVET. Why did you jump from the tower?

JOAN. How do you know that I jumped?

D'ESTIVET. You were found lying in the moat. Why did you leave the tower?

JOAN. Why would anybody leave a prison if they could get out?

D'ESTIVET. You tried to escape?

JOAN. Of course I did; and not for the first time either. If you leave the door of the cage open the bird will fly out.

D'ESTIVET [rising] That is a confession of heresy. I call the attention of the court to it.

JOAN. Heresy, he calls it! Am I a heretic because I try to escape from prison?

D'ESTIVET. Assuredly, if you are in the hands of the Church, and you wilfully take yourself out of its hands, you are deserting the Church; and that is heresy.

JOAN. It is great nonsense. Nobody could be such a fool as to think that.

D'ESTIVET. You hear, my lord, how I am reviled in the execution of my duty by this woman. [He sits down indignantly].

CAUCHON. I have warned you before, Joan, that you are doing yourself no good by these pert answers.

JOAN. But you will not talk sense to me. I am reasonable if you will be reasonable.

THE INQUISITOR [*interposing*] This is not yet in order. You forget, Master Promoter, that the proceedings have not been formally opened. The time for questions is after she has sworn on the Gospels to tell us the whole truth.

JOAN. You say this to me every time. I have said again and again that I will tell you all that concerns this trial. But I cannot tell you the whole truth: God does not allow the whole truth to be told. You do not understand it when I tell it. It is an old saying that he who tells too much truth is sure to be hanged. I am weary of this argument: we have been over it nine times already. I have sworn as much as I will swear; and I will swear no more.

COURCELLES. My lord: she should be put to the torture.

THE INQUISITOR. You hear, Joan? That is what happens to the obdurate. Think before you answer. Has she been shewn the instruments?

THE EXECUTIONER. They are ready, my lord. She has seen them.

JOAN. If you tear me limb from limb until you separate my soul from my body you will get nothing out of me beyond what I have told you. What more is there to tell that you could understand? Besides, I cannot bear to be hurt; and if you hurt me I will say anything you like to stop the pain. But I will take it all back afterwards; so what is the use of it?

LADVENU. There is much in that. We should proceed mercifully.

COURCELLES. But the torture is customary.

THE INQUISITOR. It must not be applied wantonly. If the accused will confess voluntarily, then its use cannot be justified.

COURCELLES. But this is unusual and irregular. She refuses to take the oath.

LADVENU [*disgusted*] Do you want to torture the girl for the mere pleasure of it?

COURCELLES [*bewildered*] But it is not a pleasure. It is the law. It is customary. It is always done.

THE INQUISITOR. That is not so, Master, except when the inquiries are carried on by people who do not know their legal business.

COURCELLES. But the woman is a heretic. I assure you it is always done.

CAUCHON [*decisively*] It will not be done today if it is not necessary. Let there be an end of this. I will not have it said that we proceeded on forced confessions. We have sent our best preachers and doctors to this woman to exhort and implore her to save her soul and body from the fire: we shall not now send the executioner to thrust her into it.

COURCELLES. Your lordship is merciful, of course. But it is a great responsibility to depart from the usual practice.

JOAN. Thou art a rare noodle, Master. Do what was done last time is thy rule, eh?

COURCELLES [*rising*] Thou wanton: dost thou dare call me noodle?

THE INQUISITOR. Patience, Master, patience: I fear you will soon be only too terribly avenged.

COURCELLES [*mutters*] Noodle indeed! [*He sits down, much discontented*].

THE INQUISITOR. Meanwhile, let us not be moved by the rough side of a shepherd lass's tongue.

JOAN. Nay: I am no shepherd lass, though I have helped with the sheep like anyone else. I will do a lady's work in the house – spin or weave – against any woman in Rouen.

THE INQUISITOR. This is not a time for vanity, Joan. You stand in great peril.

JOAN. I know it: have I not been punished for my vanity? If I had not worn my cloth of gold surcoat in battle like a fool, that Burgundian soldier would never have pulled me backwards off my horse; and I should not have been here.

THE CHAPLAIN. If you are so clever at woman's work why do you not stay at home and do it?

JOAN. There are plenty of other women to do it; but there is nobody to do my work.

CAUCHON. Come! we are wasting time on trifles. Joan: I am going to put a most solemn question to you. Take care how

you answer; for your life and salvation are at stake on it. Will
you for all you have said and done, be it good or bad, accept
the judgment of God's Church on earth? More especially as
to the acts and words that are imputed to you in this trial by
the Promoter here, will you submit your case to the inspired
interpretation of the Church Militant?

JOAN. I am a faithful child of the Church. I will obey the
Church –

CAUCHON [*hopefully leaning forward*] You will?

JOAN. – provided it does not command anything impossible.

 *Cauchon sinks back in his chair with a heavy sigh. The
Inquisitor purses his lips and frowns. Ladvenu shakes his
head pitifully.*

D'ESTIVET. She imputes to the Church the error and folly of
commanding the impossible.

JOAN. If you command me to declare that all that I have done
and said, and all the visions and revelations I have had, were
not from God, then that is impossible: I will not declare it for
anything in the world. What God made me do I will never go
back on; and what He has commanded or shall command I
will not fail to do in spite of any man alive. That is what I
mean by impossible. And in case the Church should bid me
do anything contrary to the command I have from God, I will
not consent to it, no matter what it may be.

THE ASSESSORS [*shocked and indignant*] Oh! The Church
contrary to God! What do you say now? Flat heresy. This is
beyond everything, etc., etc.

D'ESTIVET [*throwing down his brief*] My lord: do you need
anything more than this?

CAUCHON. Woman: you have said enough to burn ten heretics.
Will you not be warned? Will you not understand?

THE INQUISITOR. If the Church Militant tells you that your
revelations and visions are sent by the devil to tempt you to
your damnation, will you not believe that the Church is wiser
than you?

JOAN. I believe that God is wiser than I; and it is His commands
that I will do. All the things that you call my crimes have
come to me by the command of God. I say that I have done

them by the order of God: it is impossible for me to say anything else. If any Churchman says the contrary I shall not mind him: I shall mind God alone, whose command I always follow.

LADVENU [*pleading with her urgently*] You do not know what you are saying, child. Do you want to kill yourself? Listen. Do you not believe that you are subject to the Church of God on earth?

JOAN. Yes. When have I ever denied it?

LADVENU. Good. That means, does it not, that you are subject to our Lord the Pope, to the cardinals, the archbishops, and the bishops for whom his lordship stands here today?

JOAN. God must be served first.

D'ESTIVET. Then your voices command you not to submit yourself to the Church Militant?

JOAN. My voices do not tell me to disobey the Church; but God must be served first.

CAUCHON. And you, and not the Church, are to be the judge?

JOAN. What other judgment can I judge by but my own?

THE ASSESSORS [*scandalized*] Oh! [*They cannot find words*].

CAUCHON. Out of your own mouth you have condemned yourself. We have striven for your salvation to the verge of sinning ourselves: we have opened the door to you again and again; and you have shut it in our faces and in the face of God. Dare you pretend, after what you have said, that you are in a state of grace?

JOAN. If I am not, may God bring me to it: if I am, may God keep me in it!

LADVENU. That is a very good reply, my lord.

COURCELLES. Were you in a state of grace when you stole the Bishop's horse?

CAUCHON [*rising in a fury*] Oh, devil take the Bishop's horse and you too! We are here to try a case of heresy; and no sooner do we come to the root of the matter than we are thrown back by idiots who understand nothing but horses. [*Trembling with rage, he forces himself to sit down*].

THE INQUISITOR. Gentlemen, gentlemen: in clinging to these small issues you are The Maid's best advocates. I am not surprised that his lordship has lost patience with you. What does the Promoter say? Does he press these trumpery matters?

D'ESTIVET. I am bound by my office to press everything; but when the woman confesses a heresy that must bring upon her the doom of excommunication, of what consequence is it that she has been guilty also of offences which expose her to minor penances? I share the impatience of his lordship as to these minor charges. Only, with great respect, I must emphasize the gravity of two very horrible and blasphemous crimes which she does not deny. First, she has intercourse with evil spirits, and is therefore a sorceress. Second, she wears men's clothes, which is indecent, unnatural, and abominable; and in spite of our most earnest remonstrances and entreaties, she will not change them even to receive the sacrament.

JOAN. Is the blessed St Catherine an evil spirit? Is St Margaret? Is Michael the Archangel?

COURCELLES. How do you know that the spirit which appears to you is an archangel? Does he not appear to you as a naked man?

JOAN. Do you think God cannot afford clothes for him?
The assessors cannot help smiling, especially as the joke is against Courcelles.

LADVENU. Well answered, Joan.

THE INQUISITOR. It is, in effect, well answered. But no evil spirit would be so simple as to appear to a young girl in a guise that would scandalize her when he meant her to take him for a messenger from the Most High. Joan: the Church instructs you that these apparitions are demons seeking your soul's perdition. Do you accept the instruction of the Church?

JOAN. I accept the messenger of God. How could any faithful believer in the Church refuse him?

CAUCHON. Wretched woman: again I ask you, do you know what you are saying?

THE INQUISITOR. You wrestle in vain with the devil for her soul, my lord: she will not be saved. Now as to this matter of the man's dress. For the last time, will you put off that impudent attire, and dress as becomes your sex?

JOAN. I will not.

D'ESTIVET [*pouncing*] The sin of disobedience, my lord.

JOAN [*distressed*] But my voices tell me I must dress as a soldier.

LADVENU. Joan, Joan: does not that prove to you that the voices are the voices of evil spirits? Can you suggest to us one good reason why an angel of God should give you such shameless advice?

JOAN. Why, yes: what can be plainer commonsense? I was a soldier living among soldiers. I am a prisoner guarded by soldiers. If I were to dress as a woman they would think of me as a woman; and then what would become of me? If I dress as a soldier they think of me as a soldier, and I can live with them as I do at home with my brothers. That is why St Catherine tells me I must not dress as a woman until she gives me leave.

COURCELLES. When will she give you leave?

JOAN. When you take me out of the hands of the English soldiers. I have told you that I should be in the hands of the Church, and not left night and day with four soldiers of the Earl of Warwick. Do you want me to live with them in petticoats?

LADVENU. My lord: what she says is, God knows, very wrong and shocking; but there is a grain of worldly sense in it such as might impose on a simple village maiden.

JOAN. If we were as simple in the village as you are in your courts and palaces, there would soon be no wheat to make bread for you.

CAUCHON. That is the thanks you get for trying to save her, Brother Martin.

LADVENU. Joan: we are all trying to save you. His lordship is trying to save you. The Inquisitor could not be more just to you if you were his own daughter. But you are blinded by a terrible pride and self-sufficiency.

JOAN. Why do you say that? I have said nothing wrong. I cannot understand.

THE INQUISITOR. The blessed St Athanasius has laid it down in his creed that those who cannot understand are damned. It is not enough to be simple. It is not enough even to be what simple people call good. The simplicity of a darkened mind is no better than the simplicity of a beast.

JOAN. There is great wisdom in the simplicity of a beast, let me tell you; and sometimes great foolishness in the wisdom of scholars.

LADVENU. We know that, Joan: we are not so foolish as you think us. Try to resist the temptation to make pert replies to us. Do you see that man who stands behind you [*he indicates the Executioner*]?

JOAN [*turning and looking at the man*] Your torturer? But the Bishop said I was not to be tortured.

LADVENU. You are not to be tortured because you have confessed everything that is necessary to your condemnation. That man is not only the torturer: he is also the Executioner. Executioner: let The Maid hear your answers to my questions. Are you prepared for the burning of a heretic this day?

THE EXECUTIONER. Yes, Master.

LADVENU. Is the stake ready?

THE EXECUTIONER. It is. In the market-place. The English have built it too high for me to get near her and make the death easier. It will be a cruel death.

JOAN [*horrified*] But you are not going to burn me now?

THE INQUISITOR. You realize it at last.

LADVENU. There are eight hundred English soldiers waiting to take you to the market-place the moment the sentence of excommunication has passed the lips of your judges. You are within a few short moments of that doom.

JOAN [*looking round desperately for rescue*] Oh God!

LADVENU. Do not despair, Joan. The Church is merciful. You can save yourself.

JOAN [*hopefully*] Yes, my voices promised me I should not be burnt. St Catherine bade me be bold.

CAUCHON. Woman: are you quite mad? Do you not yet see that your voices have deceived you?

JOAN. Oh no: that is impossible.

CAUCHON. Impossible! They have led you straight to your excommunication, and to the stake which is there waiting for you.

LADVENU [*pressing the point hard*] Have they kept a single promise to you since you were taken at Compiègne? The devil has betrayed you. The Church holds out its arms to you.

JOAN [*despairing*] Oh, it is true: it is true: my voices have deceived me. I have been mocked by devils: my faith is broken. I have dared and dared; but only a fool will walk into a fire: God, who gave me my commonsense, cannot will me to do that.

LADVENU. Now God be praised that He has saved you at the eleventh hour! [*He hurries to the vacant seat at the scribes' table, and snatches a sheet of paper, on which he sets to work writing eagerly*].

CAUCHON. Amen!

JOAN. What must I do?

CAUCHON. You must sign a solemn recantation of your heresy.

JOAN. Sign? That means to write my name. I cannot write.

CAUCHON. You have signed many letters before.

JOAN. Yes; but someone held my hand and guided the pen. I can make my mark.

THE CHAPLAIN [*who has been listening with growing alarm and indignation*] My lord: do you mean that you are going to allow this woman to escape us?

THE INQUISITOR. The law must take its course, Master de Stogumber. And you know the law.

THE CHAPLAIN [*rising, purple with fury*] I know that there is no faith in a Frenchman. [*Tumult, which he shouts down*]. I know what my lord the Cardinal of Winchester will say when he hears of this. I know what the Earl of Warwick will do when he learns that you intend to betray him. There are eight hundred men at the gate who will see that this abominable witch is burnt in spite of your teeth.

THE ASSESSORS [*meanwhile*] What is this? What did he say? He accuses us of treachery! This is past bearing. No faith in a Frenchman! Did you hear that? This is an intolerable fellow. Who is he? Is this what English Churchmen are like? He must be mad or drunk, etc., etc.

THE INQUISITOR [*rising*] Silence, pray! Gentlemen: pray
silence! Master Chaplain: bethink you a moment of your holy
office: of what you are, and where you are. I direct you to
sit down.

THE CHAPLAIN [*folding his arms doggedly, his face working
convulsively*] I will NOT sit down.

CAUCHON. Master Inquisitor: this man has called me a traitor
to my face before now.

THE CHAPLAIN. So you are a traitor. You are all traitors. You
have been doing nothing but begging this damnable witch on
your knees to recant all through this trial.

THE INQUISITOR [*placidly resuming his seat*] If you will not
sit, you must stand: that is all.

THE CHAPLAIN. I will NOT stand [*he flings himself back into
his chair*].

LADVENU [*rising with the paper in his hand*] My lord: here is
the form of recantation for The Maid to sign.

CAUCHON. Read it to her.

JOAN. Do not trouble. I will sign it.

THE INQUISITOR. Woman: you must know what you are
putting your hand to. Read it to her, Brother Martin. And let
all be silent.

LADVENU [*reading quietly*] 'I, Joan, commonly called The
Maid, a miserable sinner, do confess that I have most griev-
ously sinned in the following articles. I have pretended to
have revelations from God and the angels and the blessed
saints, and perversely rejected the Church's warnings that
these were temptations by demons. I have blasphemed abominably by wearing an immodest dress, contrary to the Holy
Scripture and the canons of the Church. Also I have clipped
my hair in the style of a man, and, against all the duties which
have made my sex specially acceptable in heaven, have taken
up the sword, even to the shedding of human blood, inciting
men to slay each other, invoking evil spirits to delude them,
and stubbornly and most blasphemously imputing these sins
to Almighty God. I confess to the sin of sedition, to the sin of
idolatry, to the sin of disobedience, to the sin of pride, and to
the sin of heresy. All of which sins I now renounce and abjure

and depart from, humbly thanking you Doctors and Masters who have brought me back to the truth and into the grace of our Lord. And I will never return to my errors, but will remain in communion with our Holy Church and in obedience to our Holy Father the Pope of Rome. All this I swear by God Almighty and the Holy Gospels, in witness whereto I sign my name to this recantation.'

THE INQUISITOR. You understand this, Joan?

JOAN [*listless*] It is plain enough, sir.

THE INQUISITOR And is it true?

JOAN. It may be true. If it were not true, the fire would not be ready for me in the market-place.

LADVENU [*taking up his pen and a book, and going to her quickly lest she should compromise herself again*] Come, child: let me guide your hand. Take the pen. [*She does so; and they begin to write, using the book as a desk*] J.E.H.A.N.E. So. Now make your mark by yourself.

JOAN [*makes her mark, and gives him back the pen, tormented by the rebellion of her soul against her mind and body*] There!

LADVENU [*replacing the pen on the table, and handing the recantation to Cauchon with a reverence*] Praise be to God, my brothers, the lamb has returned to the flock; and the shepherd rejoices in her more than in ninety and nine just persons. [*He returns to his seat*].

THE INQUISITOR [*taking the paper from Cauchon*] We declare thee by this act set free from the danger of excommunication in which thou stoodest. [*He throws the paper down to the table*].

JOAN. I thank you.

THE INQUISITOR. But because thou has sinned most presumptuously against God and the Holy Church, and that thou mayst repent thy errors in solitary contemplation, and be shielded from all temptation to return to them, we, for the good of thy soul, and for a penance that may wipe out thy sins and bring thee finally unspotted to the throne of grace, do condemn thee to eat the bread of sorrow and drink the water of affliction to the end of thy earthly days in perpetual imprisonment.

JOAN [*rising in consternation and terrible anger*] Perpetual imprisonment! Am I not then to be set free?

LADVENU [*mildly shocked*] Set free, child, after such wickedness as yours! What are you dreaming of?

JOAN. Give me that writing. [*She rushes to the table; snatches up the paper; and tears it into fragments*] Light your fire: do you think I dread it as much as the life of a rat in a hole? My voices were right.

LADVENU. Joan! Joan!

JOAN. Yes: they told me you were fools [*the word gives great offence*], and that I was not to listen to your fine words nor trust to your charity. You promised me my life; but you lied [*indignant exclamations*]. You think that life is nothing but not being stone dead. It is not the bread and water I fear: I can live on bread: when have I asked for more? It is no hardship to drink water if the water be clean. Bread has no sorrow for me, and water no affliction. But to shut me from the light of the sky and the sight of the fields and flowers; to chain my feet so that I can never again ride with the soldiers nor climb the hills; to make me breathe foul damp darkness, and keep from me everything that brings me back to the love of God when your wickedness and foolishness tempt me to hate Him: all this is worse than the furnace in the Bible that was heated seven times. I could do without my warhorse; I could drag about in a skirt; I could let the banners and the trumpets and the knights and soldiers pass me and leave me behind as they leave the other women, if only I could still hear the wind in the trees, the larks in the sunshine, the young lambs crying through the healthy frost, and the blessed blessed church bells that send my angel voices floating to me on the wind. But without these things I cannot live; and by your wanting to take them away from me, or from any human creature, I know that your counsel is of the devil, and that mine is of God.

THE ASSESSORS [*in great commotion*] Blasphemy! blasphemy! She is possessed. She said our counsel was of the devil. And hers of God. Monstrous! The devil is in our midst, etc., etc.

D'ESTIVET [*shouting above the din*] She is a relapsed heretic,

obstinate, incorrigible, and altogether unworthy of the mercy
we have shewn her. I call for her excommunication.

THE CHAPLAIN [*to the Executioner*] Light your fire, man. To
the stake with her.

> *The Executioner and his assistants hurry out through the
> courtyard.*

LADVENU. You wicked girl: if your counsel were of God would
He not deliver you?

JOAN. His ways are not your ways. He wills that I go through
the fire to His bosom; for I am His child, and you are not fit
that I should live among you. That is my last word to you.

> *The soldiers seize her.*

CAUCHON [*rising*] Not yet.

> *They wait. There is a dead silence. Cauchon turns to the
> Inquisitor with an inquiring look. The Inquisitor nods
> affirmatively. They rise solemnly, and intone the sentence
> antiphonally.*

CAUCHON. We decree that thou art a relapsed heretic.

THE INQUISITOR. Cast out from the unity of the Church.

CAUCHON. Sundered from her body.

THE INQUISITOR. Infected with the leprosy of heresy.

CAUCHON. A member of Satan.

THE INQUISITOR. We declare that thou must be excom-
municate.

CAUCHON. And now we do cast thee out, segregate thee, and
abandon thee to the secular power.

THE INQUISITOR. Admonishing the same secular power that
it moderate its judgment of thee in respect of death and
division of the limbs. [*He resumes his seat*].

CAUCHON. And if any true sign of penitence appear in thee, to
permit our Brother Martin to administer to thee the sacrament
of penance.

THE CHAPLAIN. Into the fire with the witch [*he rushes at her,
and helps the soldiers to push her out*].

> *Joan is taken away through the courtyard. The assessors
> rise in disorder, and follow the soldiers, except Ladvenu, who
> has hidden his face in his hands.*

CAUCHON [*rising again in the act of sitting down*] No, no: this is irregular. The representative of the secular arm should be here to receive her from us.

THE INQUISITOR [*also on his feet again*] That man is an incorrigible fool.

CAUCHON. Brother Martin: see that everything is done in order.

LADVENU. My place is at her side, my Lord. You must exercise your own authority. [*He hurries out*].

CAUCHON. These English are impossible: they will thrust her straight into the fire. Look!

He points to the courtyard, in which the glow and flicker of fire can now be seen reddening the May daylight. Only the Bishop and the Inquisitor are left in the court.

CAUCHON [*turning to go*] We must stop that.

THE INQUISITOR [*calmly*] Yes; but not too fast, my lord.

CAUCHON [*halting*] But there is not a moment to lose.

THE INQUISITOR. We have proceeded in perfect order. If the English choose to put themselves in the wrong, it is not our business to put them in the right. A flaw in the procedure may be useful later on: one never knows. And the sooner it is over, the better for that poor girl.

CAUCHON [*relaxing*] That is true. But I suppose we must see this dreadful thing through.

THE INQUISITOR. One gets used to it. Habit is everything. I am accustomed to the fire: it is soon over. But it is a terrible thing to see a young and innocent creature crushed between these mighty forces, the Church and the Law.

CAUCHON. You call her innocent!

THE INQUISITOR. Oh, quite innocent. What does she know of the Church and the Law? She did not understand a word we were saying. It is the ignorant who suffer. Come, or we shall be late for the end.

CAUCHON [*going with him*] I shall not be sorry if we are: I am not so accustomed as you.

They are going out when Warwick comes in, meeting them.

WARWICK. Oh, I am intruding. I thought it was all over. [*He makes a feint of retiring*].

CAUCHON. Do not go, my lord. It is all over.

THE INQUISITOR. The execution is not in our hands, my lord;

but it is desirable that we should witness the end. So by your leave – [*He bows, and goes out through the courtyard*].

CAUCHON. There is some doubt whether your people have observed the forms of law, my lord.

WARWICK. I am told that there is some doubt whether your authority runs in this city, my lord. It is not in your diocese. However, if you will answer for that I will answer for the rest.

CAUCHON. It is to God that we both must answer. Good morning, my lord.

WARWICK. My lord: good morning.

They look at one another for a moment with uncon-cealed hostility. Then Cauchon follows the Inquisitor out. Warwick looks round. Finding himself alone, he calls for attendance.

WARWICK. Hallo: some attendance here! [*Silence*]. Hallo, there! [*Silence*]. Hallo! Brian, you young blackguard, where are you? [*Silence*]. Guard! [*Silence*]. They have all gone to see the burning: even that child.

The silence is broken by someone frantically howling and sobbing.

WARWICK. What in the devil's name – ?

The Chaplain staggers in from the courtyard like a demented creature, his face streaming with tears, making the piteous sounds that Warwick has heard. He stumbles to the prisoner's stool and throws himself upon it with heartrending sobs.

WARWICK [*going to him and patting him on the shoulder*] What is it, Master John? What is the matter?

THE CHAPLAIN [*clutching at his hand*] My lord, my lord: for Christ's sake pray for my wretched guilty soul.

WARWICK [*soothing him*] Yes, yes: of course I will. Calmly, gently –

THE CHAPLAIN [*blubbering miserably*] I am not a bad man, my lord.

WARWICK. No, no: not at all.

THE CHAPLAIN. I meant no harm. I did not know what it would be like.

WARWICK [*hardening*] Oh! You saw it, then?

THE CHAPLAIN. I did not know what I was doing. I am a hotheaded fool; and I shall be damned to all eternity for it.

WARWICK. Nonsense! Very distressing, no doubt; but it was not your doing.

THE CHAPLAIN [*lamentably*] I let them do it. If I had known, I would have torn her from their hands. You dont know: you havnt seen: it is so easy to talk when you dont know. You madden yourself with words: you damn yourself because it feels grand to throw oil on the flaming hell of your own temper. But when it is brought home to you; when you see the thing you have done; when it is blinding your eyes, stifling your nostrils, tearing your heart, then – then – [*Falling on his knees*] O God, take away this sight from me! O Christ, deliver me from this fire that is consuming me! She cried to Thee in the midst of it: Jesus! Jesus! Jesus! She is in Thy bosom; and I am in hell for evermore.

WARWICK [*summarily hauling him to his feet*] Come come, man! you must pull yourself together. We shall have the whole town talking of this. [*He throws him not too gently into a chair at the table*] If you have not the nerve to see these things, why do you not do as I do, and stay away?

THE CHAPLAIN [*bewildered and submissive*] She asked for a cross. A soldier gave her two sticks tied together. Thank God he was an Englishman! I might have done it; but I did not: I am a coward, a mad dog, a fool. But he was an Englishman too.

WARWICK. The fool! they will burn him too if the priests get hold of him.

THE CHAPLAIN [*shaken with a convulsion*] Some of the people laughed at her. They would have laughed at Christ. They were French people, my lord: I know they were French.

WARWICK. Hush! someone is coming. Control yourself.

Ladvenu comes back through the courtyard to Warwick's right hand, carrying a bishop's cross which he has taken from a church. He is very grave and composed.

WARWICK. I am informed that it is all over, Brother Martin.

LADVENU [*enigmatically*] We do not know, my lord. It may have only just begun.

WARWICK. What does that mean, exactly?

LADVENU. I took this cross from the church for her that she might see it to the last: she had only two sticks that she put into her bosom. When the fire crept round us, and she saw that if I held the cross before her I should be burnt myself, she warned me to get down and save myself. My lord: a girl who could think of another's danger in such a moment was not inspired by the devil. When I had to snatch the cross from her sight, she looked up to heaven. And I do not believe that the heavens were empty. I firmly believe that her Savior appeared to her then in His tenderest glory. She called to Him and died. This is not the end for her, but the beginning.

WARWICK. I am afraid it will have a bad effect on the people.

LADVENU. It had, my lord, on some of them. I heard laughter. Forgive me for saying that I hope and believe it was English laughter.

THE CHAPLAIN [*rising frantically*] No: it was not. There was only one Englishman there that disgraced his country; and that was the mad dog, de Stogumber. [*He rushes wildly out, shrieking*] Let them torture him. Let them burn him. I will go pray among her ashes. I am no better than Judas: I will hang myself.

WARWICK. Quick, Brother Martin: follow him: he will do himself some mischief. After him, quick.

Ladvenu hurries out, Warwick urging him. The Executioner comes in by the door behind the judges' chairs; and Warwick, returning, finds himself face to face with him.

WARWICK. Well, fellow: who are you?

THE EXECUTIONER [*with dignity*] I am not addressed as fellow, my lord. I am the Master Executioner of Rouen: it is a highly skilled mystery. I am come to tell your lordship that your orders have been obeyed.

WARWICK. I crave your pardon, Master Executioner; and I will see that you lose nothing by having no relics to sell. I have your word, have I, that nothing remains, not a bone, not a nail, not a hair?

THE EXECUTIONER. Her heart would not burn, my lord; but

everything that was left is at the bottom of the river. You have
heard the last of her.

WARWICK [*with a wry smile, thinking of what Ladvenu said*]
The last of her? Hm! I wonder!

EPILOGUE

Dream state [handwritten note in margin]

A restless fitfully windy night in June 1456, full of summer lightning after many days of heat. King Charles the Seventh of France, formerly Joan's Dauphin, now Charles the Victorious, aged 51, is in bed in one of his royal chateaux. The bed, raised on a dais of two steps, is towards the side of the room so as to avoid blocking a tall lancet window in the middle. Its canopy bears the royal arms in embroidery. Except for the canopy and the huge down pillows there is nothing to distinguish it from a broad settee with bed-clothes and a valance. Thus its occupant is in full view from the foot.

Charles is not asleep: he is reading in bed, or rather looking at the pictures in Fouquet's Boccaccio with his knees doubled up to make a reading-desk. Beside the bed on his left is a little table with a picture of the Virgin, lighted by candles of painted wax. The walls are hang from ceiling to floor with painted curtains which stir at times in the draughts. At first glance the prevailing yellow and red in these hanging pictures is somewhat flamelike when the folds breathe in the wind.

The door is on Charles's left, but in front of him close to the corner farthest from him. A large watchman's rattle, handsomely designed and gaily painted, is in the bed under his hand.

Charles turns a leaf. A distant clock strikes the half-hour softly. Charles shuts the book with a clap; throws it aside; snatches up the rattle; and whirls it energetically, making a deafening clatter. Ladvenu enters, 25 years older, strange and stark in bearing, and still carrying the cross from Rouen. Charles evidently does not expect him; for he springs out of bed on the farther side from the door.

CHARLES. Who are you? Where is my gentleman of the bed-chamber? What do you want?

LADVENU [*solemnly*] I bring you glad tidings of great joy. Rejoice, O king; for the taint is removed from your blood, and the stain from your crown. Justice, long delayed, is at last triumphant.

CHARLES. What are you talking about? Who are you?

LADVENU. I am brother Martin.

CHARLES. And who, saving your reverence, may Brother Martin be?

LADVENU. I held this cross when The Maid perished in the fire. Twenty-five years have passed since then: nearly ten thousand days. And on every one of those days I have prayed God to justify His daughter on earth as she is justified in heaven.

CHARLES [*reassured, sitting down on the foot of the bed*] Oh, I remember now. I have heard of you. You have a bee in your bonnet about The Maid. Have you been at the inquiry?

LADVENU. I have given my testimony.

CHARLES. Is it over?

LADVENU. It is over.

CHARLES. Satisfactorily?

LADVENU. The ways of God are very strange.

CHARLES. How so?

LADVENU. At the trial which sent a saint to the stake as a heretic and a sorceress, the truth was told; the law was upheld; mercy was shewn beyond all custom; no wrong was done but the final and dreadful wrong of the lying sentence and the pitiless fire. At this inquiry from which I have just come, there was shameless perjury, courtly corruption, calumny of the dead who did their duty according to their lights, cowardly evasion of the issue, testimony made of idle tales that could not impose on a ploughboy. Yet out of this insult to justice, this defamation of the Church, this orgy of lying and foolishness, the truth is set in the noonday sun on the hilltop; the white robe of innocence is cleansed from the smirch of the burning faggots; the holy life is sanctified; the true heart that lived through the flame is consecrated; a great lie is silenced for ever; and a great wrong is set right before all men.

CHARLES. My friend: provided they can no longer say that I was crowned by a witch and a heretic, I shall not fuss about how the trick has been done. Joan would not have fussed about it if it came all right in the end: she was not that sort: I knew her. Is her rehabilitation complete? I made it pretty clear that there was to be no nonsense about it.

LADVENU. It is solemnly declared that her judges were full of corruption, cozenage, fraud, and malice. Four falsehoods.

CHARLES. Never mind the falsehoods: her judges are dead.

LADVENU. The sentence on her is broken, annulled, annihilated, set aside as non-existent, without value or effect.

CHARLES. Good. Nobody can challenge my consecration now, can they?

LADVENU. Not Charlemagne nor King David himself was more sacredly crowned.

CHARLES [*rising*] Excellent. Think of what that means to me!

LADVENU. I think of what it means to her!

CHARLES. You cannot. None of us ever knew what anything meant to her. She was like nobody else; and she must take care of herself wherever she is; for *I* cannot take care of her; and neither can you, whatever you may think: you are not big enough. But I will tell you this about her. If you could bring her back to life, they would burn her again within six months, for all their present adoration of her. And you would hold up the cross, too, just the same. So [*crossing himself*] let her rest; and let you and I mind our own business, and not meddle with hers.

LADVENU. God forbid that I should have no share in her, nor she in me! [*He turns and strides out as he came, saying*] Henceforth my path will not lie through palaces, nor my conversation be with kings.

CHARLES [*following him towards the door, and shouting after him*] Much good may it do you, holy man! [*He returns to the middle of the chamber, where he halts, and says quizzically to himself*] That was a funny chap. How did he get in? Where are my people? [*He goes impatiently to the bed, and swings the rattle. A rush of wind through the open door sets the walls swaying agitatedly. The candles go out. He calls in the darkness*] Hallo! Someone come and shut the windows: everything is being blown all over the place. [*A flash of summer lightning shews up the lancet window. A figure is seen in silhouette against it*] Who is there? Who is that? Help! Murder! [*Thunder. He jumps into bed, and hides under the clothes*].

JOAN'S VOICE. Easy, Charlie, easy. What art making all that

noise for? No one can hear thee. Thourt asleep. [*She is dimly seen in a pallid greenish light by the bedside*].

CHARLES [*peeping out*] Joan! Are you a ghost, Joan?

JOAN. Hardly even that, lad. Can a poor burnt-up lass have a ghost? I am but a dream that thourt dreaming. [*The light increases: they become plainly visible as he sits up*] Thou looks older, lad.

CHARLES. I a m older. Am I really asleep?

JOAN. Fallen asleep over thy silly book.

CHARLES. That's funny.

JOAN. Not so funny as that I am dead, is it?

CHARLES. Are you really dead?

JOAN. As dead as anybody ever is, laddie. I am out of the body.

CHARLES. Just fancy! Did it hurt much?

JOAN. Did what hurt much?

CHARLES. Being burnt.

JOAN. Oh, t h a t ! I cannot remember very well. I think it did at first; but then it all got mixed up; and I was not in my right mind until I was free of the body. But do not thou go handling fire and thinking it will not hurt thee. How hast been ever since?

CHARLES. Oh, not so bad. Do you know, I actually lead my army out and win battles? Down into the moat up to my waist in mud and blood. Up the ladders with the stones and hot pitch raining down. Like you.

JOAN. No! Did I make a man of thee after all, Charlie?

CHARLES. I am Charles the Victorious now. I had to be brave because you were. Agnes put a little pluck into me too.

JOAN. Agnes! Who was Agnes?

CHARLES. Agnes Sorel. A woman I fell in love with. I dream of her often. I never dreamed of you before.

JOAN. Is she dead, like me?

CHARLES. Yes. But she was not like you. She was very beautiful.

JOAN [*laughing heartily*] Ha ha! I was no beauty: I was always a rough one: a regular soldier. I might almost as well have been a man. Pity I wasnt: I should not have bothered you all so much then. But my head was in the skies; and the glory of God was upon me; and, man or woman, I should have bothered you as long as your noses were in the mud. Now tell me what has happened since you wise men knew no better than to make a heap of cinders of me?

CHARLES. Your mother and brothers have sued the courts to have your case tried over again. And the courts have declared that your judges were full of corruption and cozenage, fraud and malice.

JOAN. Not they. They were as honest a lot of poor fools as ever burned their betters.

CHARLES. The sentence on you is broken, annihilated, annulled: null, non-existent, without value or effect.

JOAN. I was burned, all the same. Can they unburn me?

CHARLES. If they could, they would think twice before they did it. But they have decreed that a beautiful cross be placed where the stake stood, for your perpetual memory and for your salvation.

JOAN. It is the memory and the salvation that sanctify the cross, not the cross that sanctifies the memory and the salvation. [*She turns away, forgetting him*] I shall outlast that cross. I shall be remembered when men will have forgotten where Rouen stood.

CHARLES. There you go with your self-conceit, the same as ever! I think you might say a word of thanks to me for having had justice done at last.

CAUCHON [*appearing at the window between them*] Liar!

CHARLES. Thank you.

JOAN. Why, if it isnt Peter Cauchon! How are you, Peter? What luck have you had since you burned me?

CAUCHON. None. I arraign the justice of Man. It is not the justice of God.

JOAN. Still dreaming of justice, Peter? See what justice came to with me! But what has happened to thee? Art dead or alive?

CAUCHON. Dead. Dishonored. They pursued me beyond the grave. They excommunicated my dead body: they dug it up and flung it into the common sewer.

JOAN. Your dead body did not feel the spade and the sewer as my live body felt the fire.

CAUCHON. But this thing that they have done against me hurts justice; destroys faith; saps the foundation of the Church. The solid earth sways like the treacherous sea beneath the feet of men and spirits alike when the innocent are slain in the name of law, and their wrongs are undone by slandering the pure of heart.

JOAN. Well, well, Peter, I hope men will be the better for remembering me; and they would not remember me so well if you had not burned me.

CAUCHON. They will be the worse for remembering m e: they will see in me evil triumphing over good, falsehood over truth, cruelty over mercy, hell over heaven. Their courage will rise as they think of you, only to faint as they think of me. Yet God is my witness I was just: I was merciful: I was faithful to my light: I could do no other than I did.

CHARLES [*scrambling out of the sheets and enthroning himself on the side of the bed*] Yes: it is always you good men that do the big mischiefs. Look at me! I am not Charles the Good, nor Charles the Wise, nor Charles the Bold. Joan's worshippers may even call me Charles the Coward because I did not pull her out of the fire. But I have done less harm than any of you. You people with your heads in the sky spend all your time trying to turn the world upside down; but I take the world as it is, and say that top-side-up is right-side-up; and I keep my nose pretty close to the ground. And I ask you, what king of France has done better, or been a better fellow in his little way?

JOAN. Art really king of France, Charlie? Be the English gone?

DUNOIS [*coming through the tapestry on Joan's left, the candles relighting themselves at the same moment, and illuminating his armor and surcoat cheerfully*] I have kept my word: the English are gone.

JOAN. Praised be God! now is fair France a province in heaven. Tell me all about the fighting, Jack. Was it thou that led them? Wert thou God's captain to thy death?

DUNOIS. I am not dead. My body is very comfortably asleep in my bed at Chateaudun; but my spirit is called here by yours.

JOAN. And you fought them m y way, Jack: eh? Not the old way, chaffering for ransoms; but The Maid's way: staking life against death, with the heart high and humble and void of malice, and nothing counting under God but France free and French. Was it my way, Jack?

DUNOIS. Faith, it was any way that would win. But the way that won was always your way. I give you best, lassie. I wrote a fine letter to set you right at the new trial. Perhaps I should never have let the priests burn you; but I was busy fighting; and it was the Church's business, not mine. There was no use in both of us being burned, was there?

CAUCHON. Ay! put the blame on the priests. But I, who am beyond praise and blame, tell you that the world is saved neither by its priests nor its soldiers, but by God and His Saints. The Church Militant sent this woman to the fire; but even as she burned, the flames whitened into the radiance of the Church Triumphant.

The clock strikes the third quarter. A rough male voice is heard trolling an improvised tune.

> Rum tum trumpledum,
> Bacon fat and rumpledum,
> Old Saint mumpledum,
> Pull his tail and stumpledum
>   O my Ma—ry Ann!

A ruffianly English soldier comes through the curtains and marches between Dunois and Joan.

DUNOIS. What villainous troubador taught you that doggrel?

THE SOLDIER. No troubadour. We made it up ourselves as we marched. We were not gentlefolks and troubadours. Music straight out of the heart of the people, as you might say. Rum tum trumpledum, Bacon fat and rumpledum, Old Saint mumpledum, Pull his tail and stumpledum: that dont mean anything, you know; but it keeps you marching. Your servant, ladies and gentlemen. Who asked for a saint?

JOAN. Be you a saint?

THE SOLDIER. Yes, lady, straight from hell.

DUNOIS. A saint, and from hell!

THE SOLDIER. Yes, noble captain: I have a day off. Every year, you know. Thats my allowance for my one good action.

CAUCHON. Wretch! In all the years of your life did you do only one good action?

THE SOLDIER. I never thought about it: it came natural like. But they scored it up for me.

CHARLES. What was it?

THE SOLDIER. Why, the silliest thing you ever heard of. I –

JOAN [*interrupting him by strolling across to the bed, where she sits beside Charles*] He tied two sticks together, and gave them to a poor lass that was going to be burned.

THE SOLDIER. Right. Who told you that?

JOAN. Never mind. Would you know her if you saw her again?

THE SOLDIER. Not I. There are so many girls! and they all expect you to remember them as if there was only one in the world. This one must have been a prime sort; for I have a day off every year for her; and so, until twelve o'clock punctually, I am a saint, at your service, noble lords and lovely ladies.

CHARLES. And after twelve?

THE SOLDIER. After twelve, back to the only place fit for the likes of me.

JOAN [*rising*] Back there! You! that gave the lass the cross!

THE SOLDIER [*excusing his unsoldierly conduct*] Well, she asked for it; and they were going to burn her. She had as good a right to a cross as they had; and they had dozens of them. It was her funeral, not theirs. Where was the harm in it?

JOAN. Man: I am not reproaching you. But I cannot bear to think of you in torment.

THE SOLDIER [*cheerfully*] No great torment, lady. You see I was used to worse.

CHARLES. What! worse than hell?

THE SOLDIER. Fifteen years' service in the French wars. Hell was a treat after that.

Joan throws up her arms, and takes refuge from despair of humanity before the picture of the Virgin.

THE SOLDIER [*continuing*] – Suits me somehow. The day off
was dull at first, like a wet Sunday. I dont mind it so much
now. They tell me I can have as many as I like as soon as I
want them.

CHARLES. What is hell like?

THE SOLDIER. You wont find it so bad, sir. Jolly. Like as if
you were always drunk without the trouble and expense of
drinking. Tip top company too: emperors and popes and
kings and all sorts. They chip me about giving that young
judy the cross; but I dont care: I stand up to them proper, and
tell them that if she hadnt a better right to it than they, she'd
be where they are. That dumbfounds them, that does. All they
can do is gnash their teeth, hell fashion; and I just laugh, and
go off singing the old chanty: Rum tum trumple – Hullo!
Who's that knocking at the door?

They listen. A long gentle knocking is heard.

CHARLES. Come in.

*The door opens; and an old priest, white-haired, bent, with
a silly but benevolent smile, comes in and trots over to Joan.*

THE NEWCOMER. Excuse me, gentle lords and ladies. Do not
let me disturb you. Only a poor old harmless English rector.
Formerly chaplain to the cardinal: to my lord of Winchester.
John de Stogumber, at your service. [*He looks at them inquir-
ingly*] Did you say anything? I am a little deaf, unfortunately.
Also a little – well, not always in my right mind, perhaps; but
still, it is a small village with a few simple people. I suffice: I
suffice: they love me there; and I am able to do a little good. I
am well connected, you see; and they indulge me.

JOAN. Poor old John! What brought thee to this state?

DE STOGUMBER. I tell my folks they must be very careful. I say
to them, 'If you only saw what you think about you would
think quite differently about it. It would give you a great
shock. Oh, a great shock.' And they all say 'Yes, Parson: we
all know you are a kind man, and would not harm a fly.' That
is a great comfort to me. For I am not cruel by nature, you
know.

THE SOLDIER. Who said you were?

DE STOGUMBER. Well, you see, I did a very cruel thing once

because I did not know what cruelty was like. I had not seen it, you know. That is the great thing: you must see it. And then you are redeemed and saved.

CAUCHON. Were not the sufferings of our Lord Christ enough for you?

DE STOGUMBER. No. Oh no: not at all. I had seen them in pictures, and read of them in books, and been greatly moved by them, as I thought. But it was no use: it was not our Lord that redeemed me, but a young woman whom I saw actually burned to death. It was dreadful: oh, most dreadful. But it saved me. I have been a different man ever since, though a little astray in my wits sometimes.

CAUCHON. Must then a Christ perish in torment in every age to save those that have no imagination?

JOAN. Well, if I saved all those he would have been cruel to if he had not been cruel to me, I was not burnt for nothing, was I?

DE STOGUMBER. Oh no; it was not you. My sight is bad: I cannot distinguish your features: but you are not she: oh no: she was burned to a cinder: dead and gone, dead and gone.

THE EXECUTIONER [*stepping from behind the bed curtains on Charles's right, the bed being between them*] She is more alive than you, old man. Her heart would not burn; and it would not drown. I was a master at my craft: better than the master of Paris, better than the master of Toulouse; but I could not kill The Maid. She is up and alive everywhere.

THE EARL OF WARWICK [*sallying from the bed curtains on the other side, and coming to Joan's left hand*] Madam: my congratulations on your rehabilitation. I feel that I owe you an apology.

JOAN. Oh, please dont mention it.

WARWICK [*pleasantly*] The burning was purely political. There was no personal feeling against you, I assure you.

JOAN. I bear no malice, my lord.

WARWICK. Just so. Very kind of you to meet me in that way: a touch of true breeding. But I must insist on apologizing very amply. The truth is, these political necessities sometimes turn out to be political mistakes; and this one was a veritable howler; for your spirit conquered us, madam, in spite of our faggots. History will remember me for your sake, though the incidents of the connection were perhaps a little unfortunate.

JOAN. Ay, perhaps just a little, you funny man.

WARWICK. Still, when they make you a saint, you will owe your halo to me, just as this lucky monarch owes his crown to you.

JOAN [*turning from him*] I shall owe nothing to any man: I owe everything to the spirit of God that was within me. But fancy me a saint! What would St Catherine and St Margaret say if the farm girl was cocked up beside them!

A clerical-looking gentleman in black frockcoat and trousers, and tall hat, in the fashion of the year 1920, suddenly appears before them in the corner on their right. They all stare at him. Then they burst into uncontrollable laughter.

THE GENTLEMAN. Why this mirth, gentlemen?

WARWICK. I congratulate you on having invented a most extraordinarily comic dress.

THE GENTLEMAN. I do not understand. You are all in fancy dress: I am properly dressed.

DUNOIS. All dress is fancy dress, is it not, except our natural skins?

THE GENTLEMAN. Pardon me: I am here on serious business, and cannot engage in frivolous discussions. [*He takes out a paper, and assumes a dry official manner*]. I am sent to announce to you that Joan of Arc, formerly known as The Maid, having been the subject of an inquiry instituted by the Bishop of Orleans –

JOAN [*interrupting*] Ah! They remember me still in Orleans.

THE GENTLEMAN [*emphatically, to mark his indignation at the interruption*] – by the Bishop of Orleans into the claim of the said Joan of Arc to be canonized as a saint –

JOAN [*again interrupting*] But I never made any such claim.

THE GENTLEMAN [*as before*] – the Church has examined the claim exhaustively in the usual course, and, having admitted the said Joan successively to the ranks of Venerable and Blessed, –

JOAN [*chuckling*] Me venerable!

THE GENTLEMAN. – has finally declared her to have been

endowed with heroic virtues and favored with private revelations, and calls the said Venerable and Blessed Joan to the communion of the Church Triumphant as Saint Joan.

JOAN [*rapt*] Saint Joan!

THE GENTLEMAN. On every thirtieth day of May, being the anniversary of the death of the said most blessed daughter of God, there shall in every Catholic church to the end of time be celebrated a special office in commemoration of her; and it shall be lawful to dedicate a special chapel to her, and to place her image on its altar in every such church. And it shall be lawful and laudable for the faithful to kneel and address their prayers through her to the Mercy Seat.

JOAN. Oh no. It is for the saint to kneel. [*She falls on her knees, still rapt*].

THE GENTLEMAN [*putting up his paper, and retiring beside the Executioner*] In Basilica Vaticana, the sixteenth day of May, nineteen hundred and twenty.

DUNOIS [*raising Joan*] Half an hour to burn you, dear Saint: and four centuries to find out the truth about you!

DE STOGUMBER. Sir: I was chaplain to the Cardinal of Winchester once. They always would call him the Cardinal of England. It would be a great comfort to me and to my master to see a fair statue to The Maid in Winchester Cathedral. Will they put one there, do you think?

THE GENTLEMAN. As the building is temporarily in the hands of the Anglican heresy, I cannot answer for that.

A vision of the statue in Winchester Cathedral is seen through the window.

DE STOGUMBER. Oh look! look! that is Winchester.

JOAN. Is that meant to be me? I was stiffer on my feet.

The vision fades.

THE GENTLEMAN. I have been requested by the temporal authorities of France to mention that the multiplication of public statues to The Maid threatens to become an obstruction to traffic. I do so as a matter of courtesy to the said authorities, but must point out on behalf of the Church that The Maid's horse is no greater obstruction to traffic than any other horse.

JOAN. Eh! I am glad they have not forgotten my horse.

A vision of the statue before Rheims Cathedral appears.

JOAN. Is that funny little thing me too?

CHARLES. That is Rheims Cathedral where you had me crowned. It must be you.

JOAN. Who has broken my sword? My sword was never broken. It is the sword of France.

DUNOIS. Never mind. Swords can be mended. Your soul is unbroken; and you are the soul of France.

The vision fades. The Archbishop and the Inquisitor are now seen on the right and left of Cauchon.

JOAN. My sword shall conquer yet: the sword that never struck a blow. Though men destroyed my body, yet in my soul I have seen God.

CAUCHON [*kneeling to her*] The girls in the field praise thee; for thou hast raised their eyes; and they see that there is nothing between them and heaven.

DUNOIS. [*kneeling to her*] The dying soldiers praise thee, because thou art a shield of glory between them and the judgment.

THE ARCHBISHOP [*kneeling to her*] The princes of the Church praise thee, because thou hast redeemed the faith their world-linesses have dragged through the mire.

WARWICK [*kneeling to her*] The cunning counsellors praise thee, because thou hast cut the knots in which they have tied their own souls.

DE STOGUMBER [*kneeling to her*] The foolish old men on their deathbeds praise thee, because their sins against thee are turned into blessings.

THE INQUISITOR [*kneeling to her*] The judges in the blindness and bondage of the law praise thee, because thou hast vindicated the vision and the freedom of the living soul.

THE SOLDIER [*kneeling to her*] The wicked out of hell praise thee, because thou hast shewn them that the fire that is not quenched is a holy fire.

THE EXECUTIONER [*kneeling to her*] The tormentors and executioners praise thee, because thou hast shewn that their hands are guiltless of the death of the soul.

CHARLES [*kneeling to her*] The unpretending praise thee,

because thou hast taken upon thyself the heroic burdens that are too heavy for them.

JOAN. Woe unto me when all men praise me! I bid you remember that I am a saint, and that saints can work miracles. And now tell me: shall I rise from the dead, and come back to you a living woman?

A sudden darkness blots out the walls of the room as they all spring to their feet in consternation. Only the figures and the bed remain visible.

JOAN. What! Must I burn again? Are none of you ready to receive me?

CAUCHON. The heretic is always better dead. And mortal eyes cannot distinguish the saint from the heretic. Spare them. [*He goes out as he came*].

DUNOIS. Forgive us, Joan: we are not yet good enough for you. I shall go back to my bed. [*He also goes*].

WARWICK. We sincerely regret our little mistake; but political necessities, though occasionally erroneous, are still imperative; so if you will be good enough to excuse me – [*He steals discreetly away*].

THE ARCHBISHOP. Your return would not make me the man you once thought me. The utmost I can say is that though I dare not bless you, I hope I may one day enter into your blessedness. Meanwhile, however – [*He goes*].

THE INQUISITOR. I who am of the dead, testified that day that you were innocent. But I do not see how The Inquisition could possibly be dispensed with under existing circumstances. Therefore – [*He goes*].

DE STOGUMBER. Oh, do not come back: you must not come back. I must die in peace. Give us peace in our time, O Lord! [*He goes*].

THE GENTLEMAN. The possibility of your resurrection was not contemplated in the recent proceedings for your canonization. I must return to Rome for fresh instructions. [*He bows formally, and withdraws*].

THE EXECUTIONER. As a master in my profession I have to consider its interests. And, after all, my first duty is to my wife and children. I must have time to think over this. [*He goes*].

CHARLES. Poor old Joan! They have all run away from you except this blackguard who has to go back to hell at twelve o'clock. And what can I do but follow Jack Dunois' example, and go back to bed too? [*He does so*].

JOAN [*sadly*] Goodnight, Charlie.

CHARLES [*mumbling in his pillows*] Goo ni. [*He sleeps. The darkness envelops the bed*].

JOAN [*to the soldier*] And you, my one faithful? What comfort have you for Saint Joan?

THE SOLDIER. Well, what do they all amount to, these kings and captains and bishops and lawyers and such like? They just leave you in the ditch to bleed to death; and the next thing is, you meet them down there, for all the airs they give themselves. What I say is, you have as good a right to your notions as they have to theirs, and perhaps better. [*Settling himself for a lecture on the subject*] You see, it's like this. If – [*the first stroke of midnight is heard softly from a distant bell*]. Excuse me: a pressing appointment – [*He goes on tiptoe*].

The last remaining rays of light gather into a white radiance descending on Joan. The hour continues to strike.

JOAN. O God that madest this beautiful earth, when will it be ready to receive Thy saints? How long, O Lord, how long?

Saint Joan

Composition begun 29 April 1923; completed 24 August 1923. First published in German translation, as *Die heilige Johanna*, in the *Neue Rundschau* (Berlin), June–September 1924. Published in English, 1924. First presented by the Theatre Guild at the Garrick Theatre, New York, on 28 December 1923.

Robert de Baudricourt   *Ernest Cossart*
Steward   *William M. Griffith*
Joan ('The Maid')   *Winifred Lenihan*
Bertrand de Poulengey   *Frank Tweed*
Georges, Duc de la Trémouille, Constable of France   *Herbert Ashton*
The Archbishop of Rheims (Regnault de Chartres)   *Albert Bruning*
Court Page   *Jo Mielziner*
Gilles de Rais ('Bluebeard')   *Walton Butterfield*
Captain La Hire   *Morris Carnovsky*
The Dauphin (later Charles VII)   *Philip Leigh*
The Duchess de la Trémouille   *Elizabeth Pearré*
Jean, Comte de Dunois, Bastard of Orleans   *Maurice Colbourne*
Dunois' Page   *James Norris*
Richard de Beauchamp, Earl of Warwick   *A. H. Van Buren*
John Bowyer Spenser Neville de Stogumber (Warwick's Chaplain)
    Henry Travers
Warwick's Page   *Seth Baldwin*
Peter [Píerre] Cauchon, Bishop of Beauvais   *Ian Maclaren*
Brother John Lemaître (The Inquisitor)   *Joseph Macaulay*
John d'Estivet, Canon of Bayeux   *Albert Perry*
Thomas de Courcelles, Canon of Paris   *Walton Butterfield*
Brother Martin Ladvenu   *Morris Carnovsky*
The Executioner   *Herbert Ashton*
An English Soldier   *Frank Tweed*

A Clerical Gentleman   *Ernest Cossart*
Also Courtiers, Monks, Soldiers, etc.

Period – The Fifteenth Century, during the Hundred Years War. In France

Principal Works of Bernard Shaw[*]

PLAYS

Widowers' Houses (1893)
Plays Pleasant and Unpleasant (1898) (including *Mrs Warren's Profession; Arms and the Man; Candida; You Never Can Tell*)
Three Plays for Puritans (1901) (including *The Devil's Disciple; Caesar and Cleopatra*)
Man and Superman (1903)
John Bull's Other Island (1907)
Major Barbara (1907)
The Doctor's Dilemma (1911)
Getting Married (1911)
Misalliance (1914)
Androcles and the Lion (1916)
Pygmalion (1916)
Heartbreak House (1919)
Back to Methuselah (1921)
Saint Joan (1924)
The Apple Cart (1930)
Too True to be Good (1934)
On the Rocks (1934)
The Millionairess (1936)
In Good King Charles's Golden Days (1939)

NOVELS AND OTHER FICTION

An Unsocial Socialist (1884)
Cashel Byron's Profession (1885–6)
The Irrational Knot (1885–7)

Love among the Artists (1887–8)
Immaturity (1930)
The Adventures of the Black Girl in Her Search for God (1932)

CRITICISM

Major Critical Essays (1930) (including *The Quintessence of Ibsenism*,
   1891; *The Sanity of Art*, 1895 and 1908; *The Perfect Wagnerite*,
   1898)
Music in London (1931; from serialization 1890–94)
Our Theatres in the Nineties (1931; from serialization 1895–8)

POLITICAL WRITINGS

Fabian Essays in Socialism (edited, 1893)
Common Sense about the War (1914)
The Intelligent Woman's Guide to Socialism and Capitalism (1928)
Everybody's Political What's What? (1944)

* Dates are of first English-language publication.
[NB This clarification is essential in Shaw, for some of his works appeared in
translation two and three years before English publication.]

CLICK ON A CLASSIC

www.penguinclassics.com

The world's greatest literature at your fingertips

Constantly updated information on over 1600 titles, from
Icelandic sagas to ancient Indian epics, Russian drama to
Italian romance, American greats to African masterpieces

•

The latest news on recent additions to the list, updated
editions and specially commissioned translations

•

Original scholarly essays by leading writers: Elaine Showalter
on Zola, Laurie R. King on Arthur Conan Doyle, Frank
Kermode on Shakespeare, Lisa Appignanesi on Tolstoy

•

A wealth of background material, including biographies
of every classic author from Aristotle to Zamyatin, plot
synopses, readers' and teachers' guides, useful web links

•

Online desk and examination copy assistance for academics

•

Trivia quizzes, competitions, giveaways, news on
forthcoming screen adaptations

•

eBooks available to download